GENERATION ZALPHA

Connecting with the Next Micro-Generation
Maarten Leyts

Lannoo
Campus

D/2019/45/443 – ISBN 978 94 014 6379 9 – NUR 802

Cover design: Corbin Mahieu
Interior design: Atelier Steve Reynders

LannooCampus Publishers is a subsidiary of Lannoo Publishers, the book and multimedia division of Lannoo Publishers nv.

LannooCampus Publishers
Vaartkom 41 box 01.02
3000 Leuven
Belgium
www.lannoocampus.com

P.O. Box 23202
1100 DS Amsterdam
The Netherlands

Contents

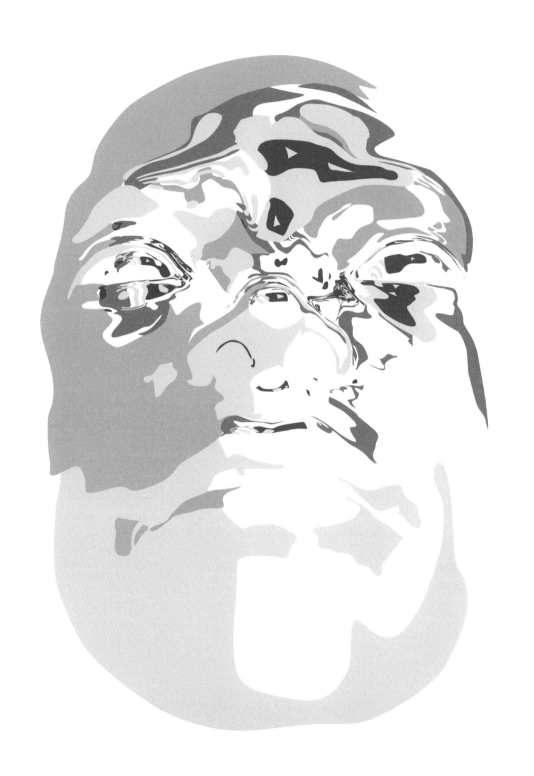

Foreword by Katryna Dow, Meeco

Every child born in today's digital world will grow up together with their digital twin. The ways in which we enable privacy for their development and security for their digital twin is as important as the rights afforded to protect them in the physical world. If we don't get this right, we risk generations born into digital slavery. *Generation ZAlpha* is a way for us to make sense of the choices we must make to ensure that risk does not become a reality.

From our first serendipitous meeting in Australia I immediately knew Maarten was a unique individual. Introduced by our mutual friend Annalie Killian with the recommendation 'you must meet' has culminated in a wonderful friendship. Maarten has become a mentor, sounding board and collaborator. Maarten immediately inspired me through his ability to share a world of possibility where young people are leading the way. His passion for why it's so important to protect their innocence, identity and future has been the foundation for what is now Generation ZAlpha.

Maarten has the empathy and insight to look at children in the way society looks at great inventors and historians. His keen eye, and interest in how kids connect, learn and communicate honours their development and insight in ways that amplify what's emerging in plain sight. Instead of dismissing early childhood development as stages, Maarten is open to how children are reshaping our society and providing a signpost for what's emerging in technology, problem solving, art, music and communication. He's both a scholar and advocate of how kids reshape the narrative for what becomes adopted, rejected and ultimately mainstream.

Kids don't have the filters or biases of adults. They are able to seamlessly move between an imaginary world where dreams are still possible and the real world. The rate of rapid technological change underscores their ideas of what will come into being. However, they are also shouldering a responsibility beyond their years in terms of the world they will inherit. Maarten has the rare quality to see children in the context of their generation; without the expectations of the world we already understand. He looks through the lens of what is unfolding, shaping and challenging society, with the ability to report what is and suspend judgement. That's what makes him a cool hunter. His ability to spot what is emerging on the fringes and then translate it into practical ways to engage with the future, always from the perspective of what is positive and possible. Regardless of the challenge, Maarten sees the insight as an opportunity to understand how to make things better. He is not one to criticise or pass judgement; his objectivity helps him spot patterns and translate what that means for the services and products of tomorrow.

The first time I heard him say 'the internet wasn't made for children' it underscored why his research, observation and insights are so important. Now almost two decades into the hyper-connected socially connected digital world and the cracks are showing. Cyber bulling, teenage depression and self-harm are on the rise.

Every day children are exposed to content for which they are not emotionally equipped. Technology is changing faster than adults can make sense of it, whilst regulation and education lag behind understanding how to protect and defend against harm.

Generation ZAlpha is a playbook for navigating these changes for marketing and communications executives, educators, regulators, advertisers, ethicists, technologists and parents.

This book provides a framework for business, government, classrooms and families to make healthy digital decisions. It provides practical ways to implement change as children move through the stages of their digital development. It's a tool to help initiate the awkward but important conversations we need to be having now to determine the wellbeing of our children tomorrow.

Foreword by the author

About four years ago, my then 8-year-old daughter sat across from me during breakfast, her eyes wide with excitement, and made a simple request: 'Daddy, can we visit Legoland in London?' The reason? Her 'friend' Max had regaled her with tales of Legoland's wonders, igniting an irresistible desire within her.

Now, you might wonder, who is this Mister Max, and why does his opinion matter so much to an 8-year-old? Mister Max, along with Miss Katy, stars in a popular YouTube family channel vlog that chronicles their everyday life, adventures, and family activities. They tackle challenges with their parents, engage in video gaming, whip up culinary creations, dabble in slime-making, and explore the latest toys. It dawned on me that these family vlogs had become a cultural phenomenon, captivating the minds of young viewers worldwide.

For those uninitiated, the fascination kids have with creating slime or watching others play video games may seem like a mystery. However, this phenomenon isn't as puzzling as it may appear. In fact, it's rooted in a fundamental mechanism of social learning: imitation. Children mirror what they see, and in today's digital age, influencers wield remarkable influence over them. These favourite influencers, primarily active on social media platforms, shape not only kids' interests but also their thought processes and even their choices in what they watch and purchase.

Family vloggers, in particular, hold immense appeal for kids. They serve as aspirational figures, not just in terms of lifestyle but also as purveyors of friendship and portrayers of joyful family dynamics. The significance of family resonates deeply with children, whether they hail from households with parents together, separated, or struggling to find moments of togetherness amid hectic work and school schedules. As long as families continue to create content, kids will remain engaged, underscoring how marketing has evolved, moving from brands to consumers through the conduit of one consumer to another.

Children are spending an ever-increasing amount of time in front of screens, where advertisements inevitably lurk. Be it on TV, within video games, or through product placements in the YouTube shows they adore, children often struggle to distinguish between content that mirrors their daily lives and advertisements. The lessons gleaned from these shows often reinforce the idea that acquiring more material possessions leads to greater happiness. Just like adults, young people tend to buy from those they trust.

Dale Kunkel, a respected expert in children and media issues and a professor of communication at the University of Arizona, found that children, up until around the age of eight, lack a full comprehension of advertising's persuasive intent. They may not grasp that marketers seek to sway their opinions or mould their thoughts in a particular direction. Steffi De Jans, a researcher focused on children's advertising literacy at Ghent University in Belgium, has highlighted that children are more susceptible to advertising than adults. This susceptibility often translates into more positive attitudes toward brands and products, sometimes prompting children to nudge their parents toward specific purchases. In a nutshell, Alphas – the generation born after 2010 – are a direct influence on the wallets of their Generation Y parents.

I founded Trendwolves roughly 15 years ago – an agency specialising in trends, futures, marketing, and innovation, with a distinct focus on youth culture (ages 12 and above). Admittedly, I was initially surprised by the extent of influence wielded by influencers within youth culture, especially among kids. The realisation hit closer to home when I saw my own children becoming targets of influence through the YouTube shows they adored. What's more, children of their age often fail to recognise these tactics as advertising. In this respect, traditional television, with its regulated advertising, seems like a safer haven for parents compared to the sometimes less-than-transparent strategies employed on the internet.

At Trendwolves, our mission is to assist governments, brands, and companies in connecting and engaging more effectively with young audiences. The ongoing debate over the compatibility of marketing and ethics is a valid one. However, it's undeniable that choices must be made, and our role is to help consumers make informed choices based on social selling. Our approach revolves around building trust, fostering co-creation, nurturing real communities, creating social value, and harnessing the Power of We. Our marketing principles are founded on transparency, responsibility, fairness, and honesty.

With this book, my goal is to delve into the value of generational thinking as well as the power of micro-generations by shedding light on this latest cohort, Gen ZAlpha, who are made up of the youngest of Gen Z and the eldest of Gen

Alpha. In the following pages, I want to introduce you to the evolving context that shapes and shaped their upbringing, their behaviour online, the watch-outs, kidfluencing, learning, technology, gaming, advertising, privacy and laws, and much more! I aim to share a more positive narrative, firmly believing that youth culture is a potent catalyst for change. So, let's embark on this journey together, as we unravel the intriguing world of Generation ZAlpha and their profound impact on our society.

Generation Alpha entered the world at the same time the Apple iPad made its debut. This isn't just a coincidence; it's the defining backdrop of their existence. More broadly, through this book, I hope to highlight how technology has played a more profound role in shaping generations than any other factor (e.g. historical events). As stated by Dr. Chromey (2019) 'It's through technology that we experience events and times.'[106] He explains that while Baby Boomers had Woodstock, Millennials were marked by '9/11 Awareness', Gen Z the climate & economic crisis and Gen Alpha by Covid-19, it's technology that truly shaped us. Across different generations, technology has shaped the way we experience those events more than the events themselves. Moreover, he says that 'without technology, we wouldn't be aware. Without awareness, we wouldn't change. Without change, we wouldn't grow. And without growth, we wouldn't have definitions of generations.'[107]

Within these pages, you'll discover a collection of insightful conversations with exceptional children and their parents from around the globe. We've delved into their digital behaviours, concerns, aspirations, the rise of kidpreneurs, and the influence of kidfluencers. This book is a reflection of their generation, offering a glimpse into their inner world for anyone seeking a deeper understanding.

Drawing from these candid discussions and our expertise in generational dynamics, this book offers a unique perspective on Generation ZAlpha, shedding light on their distinctive characteristics and the evolving landscape they inhabit. The book also deep-dives into Gen Z and Gen Alpha separately, what distinguishes them and what unites them. Let's go!

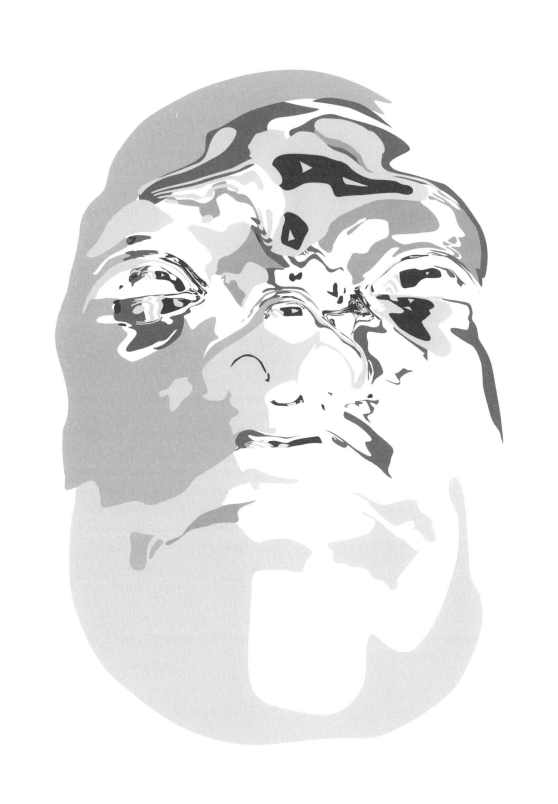

Chapter 1:
Gen ZAlpha and Generational Thinking

'I want to invent a device for getting shots easily in a less scary way', says Zy, a 10-year-old girl who is afraid of needles. Another 11-year-old, Fia, is interested in inventing a submarine for collecting waste materials from the oceans. Mylo, 11 years old, says, 'Climate change is like a snowball which is growing but it is yet small enough to control.'

Generational thinking has always been controversial. How Gen Y, Gen Z and Gen Alpha differ from each other and older generations such as the Baby Boomers or Gen X has been debated for many years. But if you talk to today's kids you will realise that they have very sharp minds with clever ideas and they are willing to act on them. In spite of social media age restrictions, parental controls and a pandemic, they are rapidly showing signs of great potential.

In this book, we are going to talk about today's kids i.e. Gen ZAlpha, the children born between the year 2006 to 2012. They are on the cusp of Gen Z and Gen Alpha. This micro-generation is the one that was most affected by the pandemic. ZAlphas are a hybrid generation of children who are the youngest of Generation Z and the oldest of Generation Alpha. They are aged between 10 and 15 and are the children of Millennials. ZAlphas are wise beyond their years. They are using their childhood experience, shaped by the climate crisis, cost of living crisis, the war in Ukraine, the pandemic and economic recession, to think productively. According to a recent study by Barnados (2022), 70% say that cost of living increases have negatively impacted their children over the past 6 months.[101] They have inherited traits such as digital nativism and a belief in social good, while rejecting time-wasting and self-deprecation on social media platforms. They are taking control of their finances and demonstrating positive money habits, with a growing interest in the pocket money economy and entrepreneurship, also known as 'kidpreneurs'. They might not be old enough yet to open their own bank accounts or drive to a store, but they are definitely steering some of their parents' purchasing decisions from what they see online in unboxing videos or other content on social media etc. Brands are smartly taking notice of this. They are also highly aware of environmental issues and are becoming our redeemers, with a staggering 45% of global youth saying that climate anxiety affects their daily lives.

The Pandemic as a Catalyst of Change for Gen ZAlpha

Professor Buller of the London Business School suggests that ZAlphas are set to reshape society in the coming years, with a focus on sustainability, social justice, and inter-generational exchange.[1] Data from a survey conducted across 20 countries (Denmark, America, Australia, Switzerland, India, Singapore, UK, UAE and others) shows the effects of the pandemic on the ZAlphas. The kids were asked to describe their feelings about the lockdown during the pandemic. The younger kids said that the inability to go and play outside was the major reason behind their frustration during the lockdown while for Gen Z the cancellation of board examinations and not being able to apply for university admissions was the difficult and frustrating part. However, the hardest part of the lockdown was not being able to see friends and go on trips. Many kids, around 53.6%, said they missed meeting their friends and family the most. About 20.9% said they missed playing sports and doing activities. Not being able to hang out with friends and do things made them feel not so good in their minds. Because of the lockdown, they didn't get to spend time with their friends or important grown-ups like teachers. Now they really want to be around people and have fun. They also saw their parents working from home, which made them think about how to balance work and other things in their lives. This pandemic experience has also impacted Alphas' screen time usage. Today, thanks to social media, that subject frequently goes viral. Whether it's a blog post or newspaper article, video interview or lecture, Gen Alpha are heavily influenced by social media and the Gen Z influencers who dominate their feeds. So events of the lockdown years will have had a significant impact on who they are. We can also say that this generation has been unofficially labelled 'Gen C', as in Generation Covid, because of how much their lives will have been shaped by this pandemic. The educational, economic, psychological and social effects of the pandemic will affect the Alphas for a longer period of time. It has left marks on their minds as they are more empathetic towards the environment and they want to talk more about social issues. They have been playing video games from a very early age which has helped create minds which take an active role in finding solutions to the problems around them. Gen Alpha kids feel a responsibility to reverse the damage caused by the older generations. They are learning empowerment and self-expression and have developed their own personal style. They know that relationships are two-way streets which is why they need to be built on trust, participation and authenticity. To understand what has shaped their thinking and behaviour, we first need to learn about generational thinking.[2]

So, Generational Thinking?

It's okay to feel different thoughts about generational thinking. Some people think it's a good way to understand generations, while others think it's not helpful. For example, when we look at different generations, we can find things they have in common and things that make them different. A 45-year-old person from Generation X might see similarities with Millennials, and a Baby Boomer might realise they share things with Generation Y colleagues. Sometimes people don't agree with the things that are said about their generation.

Meanwhile we also see patterns, values, beliefs, etc. from certain generations coming back in the younger generations. Gen Alpha are born to Millennials, hence why we call this younger cohort the mini-millennials and see them copying their parents' behaviour and brand preferences, for example. They are like a mirror to their parents (e.g. matching mother-daughter outfits) as Millennials like to offer their mini versions the things they like too (e.g. mini versions of their favourite car!). We see the same effect with Gen Z being the children of Gen X.[87]

> 'Two troubling phenomena converge in this mommy-and-me thing. There's the infantilisation of women to look like little girls and, on the flip side, [the pressure] for young girls to always look older – to wear bikinis and crop tops.'
>
> Natalia Mehlman Petrzela,
> Professor at the New School in Manhattan in an interview with WSJ.

The thing about generational thinking is that it makes general ideas and stereo-types. But these general ideas are about what's usual for a group of people. It's about what most people in a generation might do or be like. Julien De Wit, pres-ident of the Flemish Association for Students and author of 'Ge(n)eratie', also argues in his book that today we reduce and generalise people too quickly to the generation they belong to. For example, everyone aged under 25 is too young to be taken seriously, and simultaneously everyone aged above 65 is already 'writ-ten-off'.[96] But in reality, not everyone in that generation is the same. Some people might not like to be seen as a typical example of their generation. That's okay because everyone is unique. There are always exceptions to the rules. But this doesn't mean we should ignore the idea of generational thinking completely. In-stead, we can think about it as a way to understand that no one is just average.

Generational thinking is often used to explain social and cultural trends, as well as political and economic changes. In today's context, for example, we see many influencers and content creators creating depictions of the generational differ-ences in funny memes on Instagram or TikTok – most often on topics such as work, management styles and parenting. An example of this is Krian Bearney (@krianbearney) who in one of his memes on Instagram (2023) shows the dif-ferent attitudes to going to work. Other trending hashtags for this type of memes are #generations, #genzvsmillennials, #genzmemes. Meme culture in general is generally a very accurate representation of what currently lives and breathes across generations. Meme culture is also a platform for youngsters to express themselves, what they think etc. As De Wit expresses in his book, 'We don't re-ally listen to what youngsters have to say', which is also a reason why he wants to shed a light on the younger generations through his book.

@krianbearney depicts the different attitudes to work for Boomers, Millennials and Gen Z.

However, a first challenge to this approach is that it can be limiting and can lead to a narrow understanding of people's experiences and perspectives. There is more diversity within generations than between them. There are many factors that shape a person's identity and worldview, such as their race, gender, class, and upbringing. These factors can have a greater impact on a person's values and beliefs than their age or the time period in which they were born. Therefore, the author suggests that it is important to recognise the diversity within generations and not make assumptions based on age alone.

Younger generations appear to be more progressive and open-minded than older generations. While it is true that younger generations may be more supportive of certain social and political issues, such as LGBTQ rights and environmental protection, the author argues that this is not exclusive to them. There are many older people who hold progressive views, and many younger people who hold more conservative views. Therefore it is important to avoid stereotyping people based on their age and to recognise the diversity of opinions and perspectives within each generation. It can also be divisive and can lead to a lack of empathy and understanding between different age groups. By focusing too much on generational differences, we can overlook the commonalities that exist between people of different ages. For example, all generations experience the challenges of ageing, such as declining health and loss of loved ones. By recognising these shared experiences, we can build bridges between generations and foster greater understanding and empathy. Also De Wit[96] also states in his book that youngsters might pick up the 'zeitgeist' more quickly than others, but in the end each of us deals with the same insecurities and questions. One should celebrate the commonalities we all have.

A second challenge is how one defines generations. It is not about birth dates. Can you have a Millennial mindset when you were born in the late seventies? Are generational characteristics linked more with your current life stage than the era in which you were born? Your age and the things happening in your life right now can affect how you act and feel. When you graduate, find a partner, look for a job, become a parent, or lose a parent, these things will influence what you do. Your genes from your parents, your experiences as a kid, and the culture around you also play a role. But apart from your personal qualities and your childhood, the time when you were born also has an impact on your life. Events and issues of that time shape how you think and behave.

As children grow up, they change their surroundings and think about their experiences. But even then, what they do is connected to their characteristics and what they've learned from their surroundings. As they grow, things like technology, science, politics, and economics influence their thoughts and actions, not only now but also in the future. This affects everyone who's alive during those times.

Some people quickly adopt new ideas, while others take more time. But the biggest impact is on those who are young during those times. This is why they share similar values, thoughts, and traits as a generation. And just because they're moving into a different stage of life doesn't mean they'll agree with what older generations say. Often, they like to do things differently from what came before. This leads to changes in ideas and values between generations.

So yes, thinking about generations can cause disagreements. But it's a helpful way to understand and navigate our interactions with coworkers, clients, family, and others. When you see things from this perspective, it can explain why people act the way they do and help you predict how they might act in the future. But on the other hand, as we just mentioned, as a marketer it can be more interesting to celebrate what unites us, than what tears us apart and defines us differently.

The Power of Micro-Generations

Generational thinking and the surface-level categorization of each generation such as Gen X, Gen Y, Gen Z can offer very useful statistics & facts, but the desire for more specific insights is what led to this notion of hybrid generations, or micro generations. Think for example of the Xennials who bridge the gap between Gen Xers and Millennials or Zennials as in-betweeners of Millenials and Generation Z. All of these are also known as 'cuspers', or, people born at the end of one generation and near the beginning of another one. These micro groups are in unique positions: often getting a flavor of two generations in once. It is specifically beneficial for brands to be aware of this as it can help them develop even more targeted and precise strategies by knowing an even more accurate description of what the drivers, motivations and characteristics are of each sub-group. Instead of targeting children and people by age, it is even more precise to segment your target by their behaviour: everything from their passions, mindsets, values, opinions etc. Trendhunter[93] for example also talks about separating Millennials into Pro, Mid and Nouveau Millennial - as each of them grew up by experiencing different events at that time and therefore exposing different values and beliefs.

Demarcation of Generational Boundaries

Let us look more carefully at what we mean by the demarcation of generational boundaries. The generation gap is the perceived divide between different age groups in terms of their beliefs, values, and behaviours. However, The Guardian article titled 'The Big Idea: Why the generation gap isn't as wide as you think', by social researcher Rebecca Huntley,[3] challenges the popular notion that the generation gap between young and old is a vast and unbridgeable chasm. Instead, she argues that the differences between generations are not as significant as they are often made out to be and that these perceived differences are often used to create divisions between groups.

Many of the beliefs and values that are attributed to different generations are not unique to those age groups but are instead shaped by broader societal trends and historical events. For example, values associated with the Baby Boomer generation, such as their political activism and quest for social justice, were largely a response to the political and social challenges of the 1960s and 1970s, rather than something innate to that generation. Similarly, the so-called 'Millennial' values of social and environmental consciousness are not unique to that age group but are instead a reflection of broader societal trends towards sustainability and community engagement.

The differences between generations are often overstated because of the way that social media and the internet have created echo chambers in which people are only exposed to information that reinforces their existing beliefs and values. This can lead to a sense of alienation between different age groups, as each group feels like the other is living in a different world.

However, there are many areas where different generations share common ground. For example, both young and old are concerned about issues such as economic inequality, climate change, and the future of work. Many of the stereotypes that are associated with different generations are not accurate and young people are often more politically engaged and active than they are given credit for, Bobby Duffy in his book 'Generations: Does When You're Born Shape Who You Are?'[4] suggests that we should *'ditch'* these stereotypical labels.

We might say that the generation gap is an insurmountable barrier between different age groups. Instead, we should focus on the commonalities between generations and work towards creating a more inclusive and united society. By recognising that many of the differences between generations are not as significant as they are often made out to be, we can begin to break down the barriers that divide us and work towards a more collaborative and equitable future.

However, according to the French philosopher Auguste Comte, *'generational change is the key driver of the speed of societal change'*. A difference exists between the young generation and the older ones on the basis of attitude, morals, norms, values, thinking process etc. Usually, younger generations are easily adaptable to change in the society compared to the older generations.

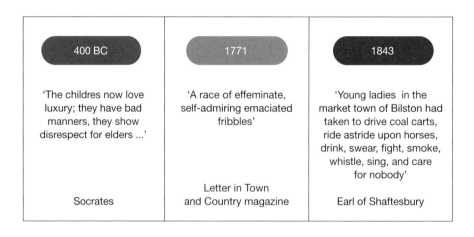

While talking about generational differences, we are more likely to create certain stereotypes about each generation that may cause *'generational conflict'*. Older generations have always looked down upon the younger ones. For example, Socrates said, in 400 BC, *'The children now love luxury; they have bad manners, they show disrespect for elders and love gossip in place of activity ...'*. I bet you can relate to this statement in today's age as well. Every older generation has been saying the same things about the younger generation since day one but now it seems more intense. One of the main reasons behind this is that in the digital age where news spreads really fast, people believe this news without even double checking the sources, which may create division. For example, if we look at the internet usage time of every generation alive today, Gen Z is at the top followed by Millennials, Gen X and then Baby Boomers at the bottom. They also show different behaviour when using the internet. This kind of difference reinforces stereotypes. Similarly, looking at how wealth is shared in the USA, Baby Boomers starting from 20% in their 30s now own almost 60% of the total wealth of the USA in their 60s (report from 2019); Generation X starting from below zero in their 20s to now up to 20% of total USA wealth in their mid 40s (as per 2019); and Millennials, starting from zero hardly even have any wealth, sitting as low as below 10% in their 30s. And for this, the Millennials are lectured by older generations. They call them excessive spenders and tell them to cancel their gym and Netflix subscriptions to save for their future property.

Generational Thinking is a powerful idea

Generational thinking is actually a very powerful idea which is often distorted by different stereotypes, myths and clichés. How we think about social generations today has been formed by the ideas of sociologists in the past. For example, Carl Mannheim, worked on formation of generational identities and how they are interlinked with the speed of change within the society. Mannheim's work was built on the theories of Auguste Comte, who described how generational change is interlinked with the speed of how we develop. Comte said ' ... our social progress rests upon death ... the successive steps of humanity necessarily require a continuous renovation ... from one generation to next' which explains the idea that generational thinking is all about changing with time. So when we reach a certain age, we stop changing or accepting change readily and that can create a generational gap.

A New View:
from Generational Thinking to Perennials

The flip side of the coin does also exist. What if the concept of generations did not exist at all? That's what Fast Company's recent blogpost (August 2023) is all about. For decades long, we have universally been following the sequential model of life: from infanthood, to school, college, work and retirement. But ever since demographics have been changing (e.g. we live longer now) and therefore what used to be seen as 'old' or 'young' before, isn't anymore. Guillen writes that 'the confluence of rising life expectancy, enhanced physical and mental fitness, and technology-driven knowledge obsolescence fundamentally alters the dynamics over the entire life course, redefining both what we can do at different ages and how generations live, learn, work, and consume together'. This generational revolution leads to the rise of 'perennials' which Serial Entrepreur says is 'an ever-blooming group of people of all ages, stripes, and types who transcend stereotypes and make connections with each other and the world around them ... they are not defined by their generation anymore.' Whereas in the not-too-distant past at most four or five generations of people coexisted at any given moment in time, now we have eight inhabiting the planet simultaneously. Guillen states that 'As longevity continues to soar, nine or ten generations may end up living together before midcentury.[88] So instead of developing generational stereotypical thinking, how can we develop a perennial mindset to all work, live and enjoy life together? Don't we all want to live and feel young as long as possible after all? Age is a mindset, so whether it's perennial or generational, why don't we go for perennial?

Losing Faith in a Better Future

We are losing faith that life will be any better for our upcoming generations than it was in our times. A survey was conducted among several countries worldwide in 2003 where people were asked, 'To what extent, if at all, do you feel that today's youth will have a better or worse life than their parents, or will it be about the same?'. The results showed that people believed in a better future at that time. In 2019, the survey was conducted again and people were asked the same question yet this time the results suggested that people have absolutely no hope left. Citizens from eight of the most developed countries i.e. UK, USA, Germany, Spain, Canada, Japan, Belgium and France believed that the future is going to be worse for the younger generations.

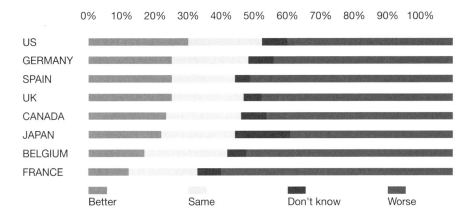

This shift in pattern from 2003 to 2019, is not about the Old vs. Young generation. It is about how we all see the future because we are all connected, ranging from the older generations to the youngest ones. We are losing optimism altogether which is alarming and challenging at the same time. These kind of things show that we have lost faith in the system and the future.

Crisis, Conflict and Decline

Some generational researchers are of the view that crisis, conflict and decline are inevitable in generational claims. This thinking is associated with a book written by William Strauss and Neil Hall entitled 'The Fourth Turning'. In this book they have identified four types of generations that repeat themselves again and again throughout history. They argued that every eighty years, there is a wrong combination of generations which leads to a crisis. Steven Bannon made a documentary[5] based on this claim and argued that we are heading towards a financial crisis. Bobby Duffy denies these claims. He argues that generational thinking is not so simple as to be defined in four repeating types; every generation is different from other generations. We can also not say that a catastrophe is about to happen because in the long term the generations' trust in politicians, satisfaction with democracy and other attitudes change very often. This ability to change shows resilience. It also shows that even after reaching the *'low point'* there is still hope because the world has already recovered from more serious crises. There is no generational effect to this claim either. Young generations usually show more trust and satisfaction in the system and politicians than the older generations but their trust diminishes with time because of the repeated disappointment with the behaviour of the politicians.

One might think that there is some generational war going on because there have been a lot of fake myths of war between generations in different contexts overall. However in reality, no generational war is brewing because the connections among the generations are very strong. The separation, however, is real. Generations and families have never been as separated in history as they are now, both digitally and physically. The younger people are moving to urban areas while older generations are staying back in the rural areas more often. The distance has an effect on other life aspects as well, for example differences in thinking or values. Then these differences start to embed division between generations and age groups. To overcome this division, we need to encourage long-term thinking and also need to support generational and intergenerational connections. Lots of stereotypes emerge from the disconnection across generations drawing them further apart. Supporting the intergenerational connections can overcome this division and sense of disconnection.

Overview of the Most Recent Generations

Let us look at the characteristics of the most recent generations. The Silent Generation (born before 1945), to a greater or lesser extent, actively went through the Second World War. They experienced the aftermath of the war and the golden years of the 1960s; they were acquainted with both hardship and wealth. They are referred to as the military generation in the USA and in Russia – for example, Mikhail Gorbachev and Ronald Reagan could be ranked among its members – while in China this was the generation of the Long March. In most countries this generation was distinguished by determination and a heightened sense of duty.

The Baby Boomers (1946–1964) mainly experienced prosperity. They lived through a time of technological innovation – television and the moon landing, to name just a few – and of the sexual revolution, emancipation, war, and civil rights. This is the generation of passionate idealists who rebelled against the institutions, the system built by their fathers. Bill Clinton hails from this generation. We find direct parallels in other countries: the war of students against the establishment in 1968, and the birth of European terrorism, the 'Red Brigades' in the 1970s. This generation has made radical politics popular. In China, it was the generation of the 'Red Guard', and the Cultural Revolution.

Gen X (1965–1979) had to battle mass youth unemployment and experienced the end of sexual freedom because of the risk of HIV. Nowadays, most of them are now balancing childcare, homeownership, and reaching the pinnacle of their careers. Indicative of Gen Y (1980–1994) is the emergence of the internet, the democratisation of mobile telephony, the fall of the Berlin Wall and the removal of internal borders within the EU. If people mention Gen Y, they visualise a generation of young people each of whom feels unique, who name all their numerous activities and roles in their profile descriptions. Hence also the name Generation Slash, referring to the forward slashes separating their various identities.

In American countries, scientists and marketers highlight a cohort that was raised by the turn of the millennium, and, therefore, they are known as Millennials. The exact definition of time boundaries differs from source to source, but the estimated dates of birth range are from 1976 to 2004. They were the first generation to experience the possibilities and uncertainty of modern life in the fast-changing world of tech.

The digital natives belong to Gen Z (1995–2009). In contrast to Gen Y, they have no recollection of a world without the internet or a world without terrorism after the War on Terror following the attacks of 11 September 2001.

In 2005, Australian demographer and TEDx speaker Mark McCrindle conducted a nationwide survey to determine the most appropriate name for the next generation.

As a result, the term Generation Alpha (2010–2025) emerged as the most popular choice.

Gen Alpha is the first generation born entirely in the 21st century, and they get their first contact with technologies at a very young age. Their association with technology made us call this generation *'More Gen Z than Gen Z'*.[6]

Alphas were born into a world with already existing laptops, tablets, and smartphones. They never lived without unlimited Wi-Fi access and modern technologies to which previous generations had to adapt. In the meanwhile, Instagram and WeChat were already present on the ubiquitous global web. For them, 'digital banking' does not exist, instead it's just 'banking'. The fact it's in the format of a mobile app is a given for them – having grown up with technology enabling all different aspects in their lives and lifestyles.

However, some experts claim that it is too early to distinguish a new generation, while others, like me, argue in favour of distinguishing those born after 2006 till 2012 as a microgeneration named Generation *ZAlpha*. This is a rising generation with first-hand experiences in the fourth industrial revolution with its artificial intelligence, XR, bionics and robotics, 5G, supercomputing, etc. Let's dig a bit deeper into this microgeneration in the next chapter.

The term Gen ZAlpha was first used by Poornima Luthra in her HR blog in 2020. Trendwolves popularised the term and brought it to the general public with their research, talks and publications. I presented about Generation ZAlpha at Retailde-tail in 2021, talking about how this new micro-generation impacts retail. The term was later also used in 2022 by Kristin Patrick, Chief Marketing Officer of Claire's.

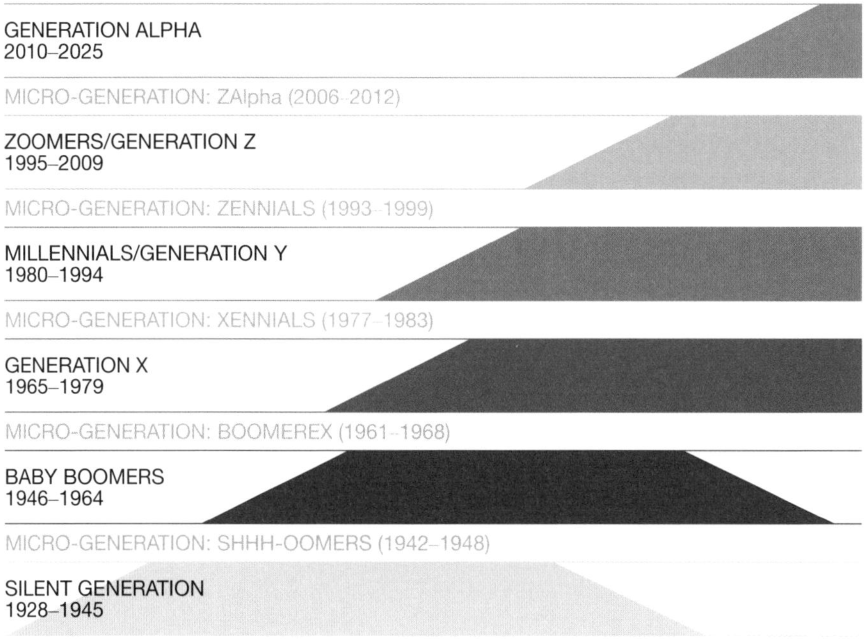

GENERATION ALPHA
2010–2025

MICRO-GENERATION: ZAlpha (2006–2012)

ZOOMERS/GENERATION Z
1995–2009

MICRO-GENERATION: ZENNIALS (1993–1999)

MILLENNIALS/GENERATION Y
1980–1994

MICRO-GENERATION: XENNIALS (1977–1983)

GENERATION X
1965–1979

MICRO-GENERATION: BOOMEREX (1961–1968)

BABY BOOMERS
1946–1964

MICRO-GENERATION: SHHH-OOMERS (1942–1948)

SILENT GENERATION
1928–1945

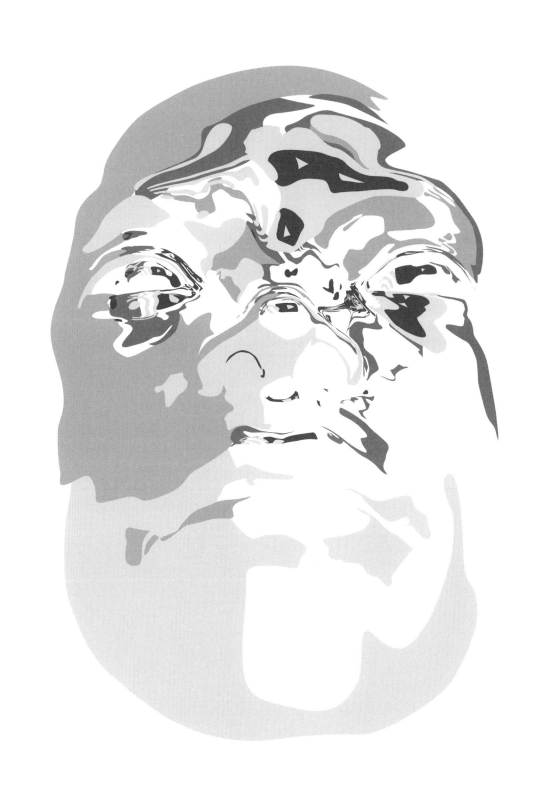

Chapter 2:
Gen ZAlpha's Childhood & Parenting Them

Before we focus on how Gen Y's parenting style connects to ZAlphas' childhood and learning , let's zoom out a bit and look at some demographics.

Population

The current world population consists of 7.98 billion people, and 1.6 billion of them were born after 2010. They are the Alphas that have almost entered their teens.

According to the United Nations (UN), by 2050, the world's population will have reached about 9.8 billion. Most of the growth in the world's population comes from the 47 least developed countries, where fertility is 4.3 children per woman. The total number of inhabitants in these countries, now 1 billion, will reach 1.9 billion by 2050. The population of 26 African countries will double in the same period.

The UN attributes the decline in the overall fertility rate to the ageing of the Earth's population. The number of people over 60 years of age is expected to triple by 2100 and reach 3.1 billion. According to the UN, from 2010 to 2015, the birth rate was below replacement level in 83 countries, which account for 46 percent of the world's population.

Africa has also seen a decline in fertility rates, from 5.1 children per woman between 2000 and 2005 to 4.4 children per woman as of 2020. At the same time, the population of Africa is gradually ageing. The UN also predicts an increase in India's population that will exceed China's population in 2024 to 1.4 billion, despite China's abandonment of the one-child policy. Also, by 2050, the USA will have lost its current position as the third-largest population of the countries, giving way to Nigeria, which is now in seventh place.

Life Expectancy

In general, as a result of the socio-economic transformations, over the past 25 years, the global average life expectancy has increased, despite the tendency toward environmental deterioration. According to a Eurostat study from 2020, the life expectancy of a newborn in the European Union was 80.4 years, which reflects the improvement in living standards and quality of life. Madrid (85.2 years) reached the highest level of life expectancy in the EU, while the lowest number was recorded in Bulgaria, Severozapaden (73.3 years).

The average age of people around the world varies, but most experts agree that people are living longer everywhere. Because more children are growing up, women are having fewer babies than they used to. This is causing the global population to gradually become older.

Multiple Generation Homes

During the mid 90s, around 5.7 percent, which is about 4 million kids, lived with multiple generations in one household. Twenty years later, this number increased to 9.8 percent, which is about 7 million children. These findings are important because they show a strong connection between how children live, how well off they are, and what effects this has on their lives in the long term.

Even though families with different generations living together are more common among groups that have less money, like young or poor mothers, the number of families with grandparents, parents, and kids all living together has grown the most among well-off groups – older, wealthier, and more educated mothers.

Changes in the different races and backgrounds of people in the country also explain why there are more families with multiple generations living together. This caused the increase in the number of families living together. Also, more people are getting extra money from the government, which helped this trend. Kids and grandkids might move in with grandparents who are financially stable.

Another reason for this increase is the relationship status of parents. There are fewer married couples and more single parents, which led to more families with grandparents, parents, and kids all living together in one place.

Parents of Gen ZAlpha

When previous generations had children, they said goodbye to their young lives. Previously, brand-new parents used to feel 'older' in one fell swoop. The Gen Y parents (parents of Gen ZAlpha) as a generation stays young and preferably will for many more years. They maintain their style and do not put their hobbies or interests aside.

To Gen Y, maturing as a parent does not mean growing old. They continue their active living, but now with one or more children in tow. These new parents still let their hair down every so often, be it with the children and friends or alone.

> 'All of the stories we write, shoot, and edit ourselves. Dad does the shooting and editing. Mom helps with costumes, props, and scripts.'
>
> says Buck,
> the father of Gabe and Garett, from California,
> who have 1.7m followers on their YouTube channel.

Gen Y is more than just a mum or a dad. In previous generations, women were expected to be a mum in the first place, and everything else was secondary. It was different for men because their job and fatherhood predominantly defined them. With Gen Y men and women, the role of mum or dad comes alongside the other positions, although priorities may change depending on the time and context.

As these new parents do not identify with previous generations of parents in any way, they do not like to be addressed as only a mother or father. They are more than that, also because there are too many dreary connotations with the parents they do not want to be.

A Look Inside Gen Y Families & the Framily

In their book *Framily – How Millennials are Redesigning Family*, Trendwolves authors Filip Lemaitre and Amélie Rombouts described the characteristics of Gen Y parents and their changing attitudes to family and parenting.

Gen Y is a fascinating group of people who have grown up with the advent of the digital revolution. They were the first group of young people with a mobile phone and MP3 player. They created their first digital profiles on MySpace and Netlog. At the start, they chatted to their heart's content using ICQ and MSN. They were the driving force behind the success of Facebook and have since created accounts on Pinterest, Twitter, Tinder, Instagram, and LinkedIn, all social media channels they master with ease. With their individualistic attitude, they are sometimes less flatteringly referred to as Generation Me.

Those who would rather not use age limits to demarcate Gen Y prefer to focus on typical values and characteristics. If people say Gen Y, they see before them a generation of young people who each feel unique. Gen Y demonstrates this by naming all their numerous activities and roles in their profile descriptions. Hence also the name Generation Slash, in reference to the forward slashes separating the various identities in those posts. These young people like authenticity and transparency. They are adept at developing digital networks. They are experienced technology enthusiasts. They strive for a large degree of efficiency and lack patience; they want to be helped quickly and precisely. They have flexible attitudes and expect the same from those around them.

They are also described as creative, as DIY fans – after all, you can learn anything from internet tutorials – and they are continually looking for a new passion, dream or talent. In the workplace, they take to a horizontal structure like a duck to water. Rather than having a boss who dictates a list of duties, they prefer a mentor who teaches them the basics, shows them the way and steers them when necessary. Gen Y-ers are generally born team players who are happy to share. On average, they are better informed, better educated, more entrepreneurial, and more critical than previous generations.

Reading this, they could be mistaken as superhuman. However, Gen Y-ers are also considered egocentric and lazy, often overestimating themselves and being exceptionally narcissistic and spoiled. They are supposedly an unhappy generation too, because throughout their childhoods they were told they could achieve anything they wanted, as long as they were prepared to work for it.

Come what may, youngsters grow into adults. They find a job, a sweetheart, leave the parental home, and, in many cases, start their own families. For previous generations, starting a family signifies the end of an era; bye-bye youth, hello responsibilities! Of course, the core family still exists, but you also see single-parent families resulting from stranded relationships, and parents who consciously chose to have a child without having a relationship. There is also a big chance that one of the parents will not be the biological father or mother of the children in the family; it is no longer an exception or a taboo. You may also know gay or lesbian couples with a child, families from a migration background or two different cultures, expats or adventurers with children, or two parents with a significant age difference.

How ZAlphas' Parents Stay Young and Active

ZAlphas' parents, i.e. Gen Y are redesigning the family dynamics. The new young parent is not prepared to put their own needs and desires on the back burner when he or she becomes a father or mother. Millennial mums are more than a mother and employee; they want to make time for themselves too, and for their friends and partner. The new young fathers do not experience their role from the sidelines, as they all too often watched their Baby Boomer fathers and the young fathers of Gen X do. If necessary, they go to their employer asking if they can work less or not at all during the hours they need to look after their son or daughter. Caring for the children is teamwork, and the stereotypical ideas about gender no longer apply.

Gen Y-ers realise better than anyone what it means to sit on the sofa in front of the TV waiting for a parent to arrive home exhausted. They want to save their children from that experience. They live in the present. Compensating for that missed time later with a day trip or the latest game is not an option for these young parents. The major pedagogical theories are lost to them. They will find out by themselves from their network. 'As long as they are happy' is the most common answer given by these young parents when you ask them how they see their children's future. After all, no one knows what will be hot in the job market tomorrow.

Just like their parents, Gen Y-ers also hold on to their lifestyle linked to youth culture. They continue to feel young and act young. Of course, there are their friends, both online and offline, whom they continue to meet up with. A number of those friends who become closely involved with the family unit even make it to the 'framily'. Family units can fall back on this network to keep their lives on track in the way they planned.

This new phase of life brings new needs with it. Brands are well aware of this and marketers focus en masse on this new group of consumers. However, if they think they will be dealing with docile consumers, they are sorely mistaken. Gen Y-ers see straight through crude marketing. Those that are only after their cash and that will not make their life any easier can forget it.

Everyone who has one or more children knows that it is not all sunshine and roses. The unwritten rule was that you should not shout that from the rooftops, at least until these new young parents came along. Gen Y-ers tell it how it is. There is no hypocrisy, and they do not mince their words. If their baby keeps them awake for the third night in a row for no apparent reason, they are not shy to call them 'little fuckers' on Facebook on occasion.

With that, we touch on a sore point for this generation: social media. Although it's hard to get them off Facebook, WhatsApp, and Instagram, they are more restrained about sharing their children on the internet. The same applies to technology. They would rather see their children climbing trees than swiping on a tablet. Gen Y clearly added its touch to the family format. Previous generations were still more likely to mirror their childhood family situation than this generation of new parents. Besides their personality traits, it is evident that they incorporate more generational traits into their family than we have been used to seeing in the past. Does that mean the family of the next, new generation of young parents will again take on a different guise? We assume it will.

Gen ZAlpha's Childhood from an Anthropological Perspective

There is no doubt that a child's development is determined by critical childhood years. At first sight, nothing would indicate that this would be any different for ZAlphas, but psychologically, they have evolved in their little universe. Despite their all-hands-on-deck attitude, they will need all their mental capabilities, because technological breakthroughs have increased possible multitasking.

In the childhood of a Millennial, there were just a dozen cartoons and a few magazines once a month. On the other hand, Alphas have access to thousands of them through their mobile phones and tablets, and every single day new ones are added. A TV commercial that twenty years ago was sixty seconds long now lasts six seconds. The average time to view a post on Instagram is less than a second. A second is a time during which a person now evaluates almost any content. That is why children are so good at a critical assessment of messages – they cannot afford to waste time on what is irrelevant for them.

It seems that this will be the first generation that can afford it, and bots will take over all the tedious tasks. Text gives way to pictures, infographics and emoticons. Visual language is taking over. The brain needs to somehow cope with eight hours and more of information consumption per day.

Technology-Based Parenting

It is easy to predict that the future of parenting will be more technologically oriented. Based on the devices and achievements that are already present in the market, it can be assumed that what usually happens in sci-fi literature and movies may soon become a reality.

We can imagine that in the future, children in kindergarten will be using devices that collect data to plan their activities. Infants will be profiled while still in the womb, and technology will also find out how to create the healthiest baby.

Today, manufacturers of children's goods and toys respond quickly to customer needs. With the growth of technological devices and developments (e.g. Moonbug example), the future of technology-based parenting is now a very likely scenario. Already, there are many individual devices and tools for infants, toddlers, kindergartens, and parents. Brands like Moonbug are helping to educate and entertain Gen Alpha through their content, with the goal of offering educational content that expands 'kids' worlds and minds'.[90]

Moonbug is seen as 'Edutainment' for Gen Alpha kids. While the likes of Amazon, Netflix, and Disney battle for streaming supremacy among adult and teenage viewers, Moonbug has found success by focusing on a younger audience. Boasting billions of views across platforms, it's positioning itself as the ultimate place for kids' educational content. (Canvas8, 2022)

However, these improvements might also lead to imbalances in society. First, not everyone can afford to buy the smart devices available today, and the situation is likely to remain the same in the near future. Parents who do not have the money for all the gadgets could suffer from the reality of raising their kids. There will be dysfunctional families, which results in the broader gap between children from low-income and high-income families.

Secondly, technology is also not well protected. Devices may not work correctly and may require constant updating. These issues create potential safety problems that can harm children, which can lead to new types of questions that parents will have to deal with in a technology-oriented world.

Online Presence Since and Before Birth

Although many toddlers and kids do not have this conscious opportunity to take a position on whether they want to post their photos and videos on social media, their parents manage it for them. These days, it is relatively common that children are disappointed that their parents are 'sharenting' – sharing their photos without their consent.

'It's weird seeing myself up there, and sometimes there are pics I don't like about myself ... then I realised I was making an impression, and I was an actual person online too, through (my mother's) page', says Cara, 11 years old. She hopes that in the near future she'll build a relationship with her mom where she'll be able to tell her true feelings about posting her pictures online in order to reach an agreement or maybe have veto power to decide what or what not to post. 'My friends will always text or tell me, like, "OMG that pic your mom posted of you is so cute", and I'll get self-conscious,' she said.

Unlike Cara, there are also examples of kids who had an opposite reaction when they discovered their digital presence. To them, it sounds very cool to be famous and popular when they are discussed among their peers and friends.

This is not only in the case of obsessive bloggers that create their 'weblog', but also with ordinary parents. In today's era of prevailing technology, almost everyone has an account on social networks, where most often parents ask for advice from fellow parents on how to properly care for a child and what to feed them. Most (more than a quarter of) children have an online presence and identity before they are actually born; parents may share, for instance, prenatal sonogram scans etc. thus making 92 percent of toddlers appear in digital reality before the age of two.

This online presence might be dangerous as well because once the photo is uploaded, the owner loses direct control over it. Photographs can be effortlessly downloaded for third parties' usage without prior approval, and be reposted, seemingly without any consent. Nowadays, the digital history of a human being should take more consideration to avoid future confusion with ageing children.

In her blog 'Sharenting', Sarah Bregel[7] discussed an app named 'Footprint' that offers an alternative method for parents to share information and pictures of their kids. As explained above, 'sharenting' has raised some privacy risks and over-exposure of kids and, in response to these concerns, 'Footprint' provides parents with a safer and more controlled way to share memories with their children. On this app, parents are encouraged to share their memories with a limited number of close friends and family instead of sharing publicly on social media. This empowers parents to have control over who can access their kids' information and images. Enhanced privacy is one of the primary advantages of using this app, especially keeping in view the potential of hackers for misusing personal information. By adopting a more private approach, parents can mitigate these risks and maintain a safer online presence for their children.

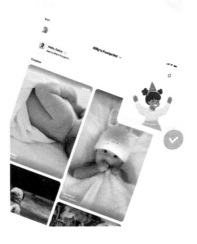

'Footprint' also allows parents to have control over the algorithms and advertising. They can control their children's online presence in a way that aligns with their values and beliefs. This can have a positive impact on children's lives and also help in protecting them from manipulation and exploitation.

The app also facilitates more meaningful connections between parents and their loved ones. By sharing updates and memories exclusively with close friends and family, parents can foster a sense of intimacy and strengthen their relationships. This controlled sharing environment encourages genuine engagement and interaction, promoting a sense of community and support.

Uncommon Technology Usage

Gen ZAlpha is growing up with a lot of exposure to technology. Smartphones and tablets are not new or surprising for them. This means they play, learn, and talk in new ways. They were born into a world where things like gadgets are really smart, everything is connected, and the real world mixes with the digital world. The things that seem new or strange to older people will be normal for them as they grow up. This is how it's been with new technology throughout history.

For a long time, our brains have been developing by interacting with the real world. In recent years, kids have been using digital devices more for learning and playing. People are wondering if this helps kids learn better or if it actually stops their development, like some scientists say. We don't really know how technology is affecting young minds yet. Some brain experts think that their way of thinking might be a bit different from how people used to think. Their worlds will mix the physical world and the digital world so smoothly that Gen ZAlpha will get annoyed if their needs aren't met quickly.

People who try to predict the future have two different ideas. Some think that modern gadgets, especially smartphones, will make us act like zombies, or they'll make us self-centred and badly behaved. On the other hand, some say that technology is making us smarter than we thought we could be. It's also freeing our minds from boring tasks so we can think about more important things. One thing is for sure: technology will not only change how Gen ZAlpha sees the world, but it will also shape who they become.

Even though it might sound worrying sometimes, we don't need to think that Gen ZAlpha's need for new technology is a big deal. They're naturally and quickly learning things like solving tricky problems, working well with others, and thinking carefully. These are important skills they'll need in the future, according to what the World Economic Forum said according to the World Economic Forum's definition of success in 2020. The promising figure below also points out that Gen Alpha's specific new skill set will lead to the development of new jobs that don't exist today.

> # 65% of Gen Alphas will work in jobs that don't exist today.[89]
>
> (Explodingtopics.com, January 2023) Technology: Putting Mental Ability At Risk?

The widespread use of gadgets means that almost everyone now has access to a computer at arm's length. There is nothing wrong with having most of the world's knowledge available to us, and this is a huge benefit in many day-to-day situations.

Although technology helps to develop specific mental capacities, existing literature shows some caveats against harmful consequences as well. Almost everyone has a powerful computer at their fingertips, which also means that we no longer need to use the same memory thinking skills to solve problems. This evolution might cause humanity to lose some of its existing mental abilities.

'Now, a person can operate pretty successfully in life, even in high-level jobs, by simply being really good at looking up answers,' says Michael Merzenich, a professor emeritus neuroscientist at the University of California in San Francisco.

On the Net, there is the possibility of losing the ability to think in a consistent, structured manner. If you are bombarded with a multitude of data, but you avoid the mental work to connect them, they remain a fragmented set of facts. Consequently, the brain begins to be lazy, and our understanding of causation diminishes. By consuming information that is not interrelated, a person can fall into an informational trance.

About Learning

Families are really important because they're where young kids start to learn important things. These things help them get ready for school and life. Families teach kids how to talk, how to work together, and how to do different tasks. When kids are little, their parents' kindness, how well they pay attention to them, and how they take care of them show how good their parenting is. These things affect how kids talk, solve problems, understand things, and get along with others.

How much kids know and the words they use depend on how rich their family is and how their mom talks to them. Kids from families with more money usually know more words than kids from families with less money. This gap keeps getting bigger. So, by the time kids are three years old, kids from richer families know about three times more words than kids from families with less money.

Benefits of Boredom

A child's non stop boredom is mostly considered a bad thing. New research conducted by Gallup shows that nearly one in five British parents fully agree that from time to time, children will be bored.

Many psychologists argue that the lack of play is at the heart of why the younger generation is growing more oppressed than the previous ones. Therefore, it is more stressful for children to solve their problems and to get along with peers, which is often the case, due to the lack of simple game experience. The lack of advanced social skills gives uncertainty and can lead to other problems with peers.

The problem is that parents think that boredom is the worst thing that can happen to a child while researchers see it as a positive thing to do to develop their creativity and define their interests.

Brain Development in the Digital Age

A child's brain grows little by little as they experience different things. The things they do and learn affect how their brain forms and works. The way their brain is built and how they learn from their experiences are connected. This means changes in how they do things when they're very young, like using lots of technology, can change how their brain grows. The skills they learn can get better because of technology, like playing video games or using the internet. But sometimes, spending too much time with screens can also make some skills not as good.

A scientist named Michael Merzenich noticed that people's brains are getting more specialised. A long time ago, people knew a lot of different things to survive. But now, our brains focus on specific tasks. This might continue for Generation Alpha, the kids born now, because of changes in how we work. Many jobs might be done by machines, so these kids will need to learn special skills to find good jobs. This could lead to some people having important jobs and others not finding meaningful work.

Imitation & Mimicking

Children learn a lot by copying others. They also connect things they know in one situation to another. This helps them learn even from things they haven't actually seen. They might learn something from a game and then use it in real life. This can be good, like learning how to take care of animals from a game about zoos. But it can also be bad, like learning to hurt others from playing war games.

Discussing 'kidfluencers' with Anna Komok, marketing and PR manager at HypeAuditor – an influencers' measurement tool – she described a 'language bot mimicking' trend. Responses of young children on social media are quick, unpolished, and most of the time, copy-paste the language of bots built for marketing purposes.

Learning Through Technologies

ZAlphas no longer need to run to their parents with each question, because the information is available within arm's reach. In one study, videos and games were approved by parents not only because of the content, but because they encourage their children to learn different languages and cultures.

'She browses YouTube and very persistently listens to other kids, for example, from America, from Finland, from who knows where, kids of her age talking about what they do, what their lifestyle is, how their life goes by day by day.' (Bulgarian mother about her daughter)

> 'For young people growing up now, new skills are just a YouTube tutorial away; there are dozens of apps to help you pick up new languages.'
>
> says Alina Morse
> 14-year-old kidpreneur, speaker, inventor, & CEO, Zollicandy

British and Dutch studies of preschoolers showed that between the ages of five and seven, children fully master the skills of working with touch screen gadgets (swiping, tapping, navigating to desired apps). However, these skills do not mean that kids have enough capability to analyse the content; parents still have a crucial role to 'safeguard' and clarify to help Alpha kids discover the world. This 'media tutor' action allows children to get used to technology and demonstrates the model of good digital behaviour.

> 'I used to sit there with him because when he starts, he opens one page and sees another ... So, he follows the thread [of links] in a very innocent way, but I realise that there are points that deserve attention. This is why I am always there. With my oldest, I check and teach him, explain to him what he is looking for.'
>
> (Italian mother of 6- and 8-year-old boys
> helps to discover Pokémon)

The latest thinking reflects that there is a crucial need in digital parenting: digital support from parents. Otherwise, it is more challenging to build a healthy digital parent-child relationship and communication.

Goalsetter is a gamified money app that encourages open family discussions about personal finances and helps educate young people to improve their financial literacy. The app also uses memes and colourful graphics to make the learning process fun and accessible.[99]

'It is important to have trust, even about something that has frightened him, even about something that he liked, just to come and share it, because that, I think, is very important.'

Misuse of Digital Technologies

Teachers also talked about issues with how students use digital tools and said that teachers need more training to fix these problems. In 2018, the French Parliament passed a law that says students aged 3 to 15 years can't use smartphones or other devices that can connect to the Internet, like tablets, in school.

'We know today that there is a phenomenon of screen addiction, the phenomenon of bad mobile phone use ... Our main role is to protect children and adolescents. It is a fundamental role of education, and this law enables it,' says Minister of Education Jean-Michel Blanquer on French news channel BFMTV.

What's Next?
Future of How Children (can) Learn

Scientists try to warn teachers about the new wave of students who will come to preschool institutions and colleges with unique views and perception of information after they have grown up on modern technologies. Nowadays, outdated methods often cause indifference to children.

Current standards should remain focused on igniting a child's potential, to be relevant for self-realisation in the context of the Latin roots of the word 'education'. 'Educare' means to train and to bring to light. New technologies allow each student to choose their own learning path. Parents and teachers can develop curricula that will enable each student to keep their way of forming value.

First, education programmes for kids should change, and educational institutions should rethink how classrooms look and feel. Industry and non-formal learning networks should join forces and play a significant role in the learning curriculum to encourage a diversity of experience.

The role of education is extraordinary. The best approach to prepare Gen ZAlpha might be to stimulate their hunger for learning and further develop critical thinking and problem-solving skills. Probably children should be taught metaknowledge: how to learn, how to keep attention, how to retain memory, how to cope with the information flow, and how not to go crazy with all this.

There is a high probability that within several decades, education will be specifically adapted to the needs of the child, and will offer thoroughly professional learning throughout life. The word 'graduation' as an event may become meaningless since, in the world of technological progress, lifelong learning becomes essential.

Schools Without Technologies

The Waldorf School is an outstanding example of a school with neo-humanistic approaches to learning. Many tech experts of Silicon Valley (eBay, Google, Apple, Yahoo, Hewlett-Packard) sent their children to this school.

Teachers encourage students to learn the subjects by expressing themselves through artistic activities, such as drawing, rather than consuming information that is uploaded on a tablet.

In technology-free schools, the approach centres on the belief that digital devices limit creative thinking, interaction, and attention of people, and have no place in the upbringing of young children. The classrooms in Waldorf Schools are also designed to make students feel comfortable and secure. The purpose is to eliminate the distraction of electronic media to encourage more communication between teacher and student during lessons.

One of the reasons why parents in the digital industry choose technology-free education for their children is because it teaches students innovative thinking skills. The fact that parents working for advanced technology companies question the value of computers in education makes us wonder whether the futuristic dream of high-tech schools is in the interests of the next generation.

AI Tutors or Human Teachers; Which is Better?

A school in Silicon Valley is utilising AI tutors developed by OpenAI. These AI tutors are designed to assist students with their learning and provide personalised educational support. The school believes that AI technology has potential to enhance the learning experience and improve educational outcomes for students.

The AI tutors developed by OpenAI use machine learning algorithms to adapt to each student's individual needs and provide tailored instruction. They can analyse student performance data and generate personalised feedback, helping students identify areas for improvement and offering targeted guidance. The AI tutors also have the ability to answer questions and provide explanations, serving as virtual tutors available to students at any time.

The school's implementation of AI tutors aims to address the challenges of limited resources and overcrowded classrooms. By leveraging AI technology, the school hopes to provide students with personalised attention and support that may be difficult to achieve in traditional classroom settings. These AI tutors aim to enhance the learning experience by providing personalised instruction and support to students.

However, there are also some potential concerns surrounding the use of AI in education. While the implementation of AI in education shows promise, questions remain about the role of human teachers and the extent to which AI can replicate their qualities. The extent to which AI tutors can replicate the benefits of human interaction and personalised teaching is debatable. Critics argue that human teachers offer unique qualities such as empathy, adaptability, and emotional connection that AI tutors may not be able to fully replace.

My advice to young people is to put down their phones.
Don't think that it's okay to live in your phone.
You have a lot more to say than Instagram.
And a lot to experience in the real world.
And the most important thing is standing in front
of another person
And feeling empathy for them.
That can't be done on a phone.
I hope young people will take some power also
Going to the streets and fight for what they believe in.
And good luck.
I'm sorry for young people that there are these
existential disasters looming.'

Nan Goldin's advice to the young

Chapter 3:
Characteristics of Gen Alpha

Who Are They?

Time to zoom in on Gen Alpha specifically. The latest in the queue of demographic cohorts, Alphas are the most transformative generation so far. They are not the first digitally native generation (Gen Z is) however, they are the fastest at understanding and most rapidly growing generation in the digital age along with all its technological advancements, and it is all they know if they are to socialise, work and live. As described before, Gen Alpha is the first generation to be born in the 21st century, and will reach adulthood by 2031. In 2024, the oldest Alpha child is 14 years old, and given the evolution of technology and the previously mentioned population growth of children towards 2025, it is predictable that this generation will transform mankind's way of life. An average child nowadays has 100 photos on social media even before reaching the age of 1 year. They are heavy users of the internet before they're even toddlers. Events such as the release of Minecraft, the release of Alexa and Echo Smart Speakers as well as worldwide climate strikes and the cost of living crisis have shaped their upbringing. That is why more and more sociologists, psychologists, and marketers all over the world are trying to identify and classify the characteristics of this youngest of generations.

Most Tech-Intensive & Educated Generation

The eldest Alphas are about to enter into their teen years, which makes this time perfect to study their behaviors for marketing purposes. They are heavy technology users just like their predecessors and even though both reality and virtual world are similar for them, they prefer the virtual world over the reality. In 2021, a 19% increase was noticed in the watch time of online videos. This is supposed to increase. They will also want the brands to engage with them through this technology. Marketers need to personalise interactive video messages if they want to target the generation in an effective way.

> '54% of Gen Alpha kids own tablets – and they watch a lot of streaming video content, mostly on YouTube, Disney+, and Netflix, the survey found.'[91]

A Common Sense Media report states that almost every seventh parent assumes that social media helps their Gen Alpha children to learn, and in parallel, Psychology Today claims that time behind the screens can help children over two years of age to develop coordination and quick reaction skills. On the flip side, due to ubiquitous technologies and the rapid spread of screen usage from an early age, experts report possible delays in speech development and slow social development.

> 'My generation is quite happy. Now many of my peers have enough pocket money every month, and their learning conditions are very good, so they can ask teachers in remedial classes on weekends if they don't understand. Some parents even quit their jobs to study with their children!'
>
> Sunny Liu.
> Shanghai, China

Generation Alpha has all the possibilities to be the most tech-intensive and educated generation yet. They grow and actively develop in the digital emerging world of technology, which for previous generations seemed impossibly complicated.

'... We're never more than a few Google searches away from learning about anything going on in the world! It's hard to say whether that makes us more equipped than previous generations to take on more responsibilities at a younger age, just because it's such an unprecedented situation ...'

Alina Morse
Teenpreneur, speaker, inventor, & CEO, Zollicandy

Most Diverse & Inclusive Cohort

The globalisation of the world, increased international migration and life expectancy, gender equality, LGBTQ+ parenting and women's empowerment makes this generation the most diverse generation ever. They are expected to be more open to cross-cultural partnerships and families. This generation is all about inclusion and will engage with the brands that care about humanity. Reports show that 72% of people worldwide like to buy from brands that show diversity and inclusion and if they're sure that the brand they're buying from, supports their values, their customer loyalty increases by 80%. To target this generation, brands will have to reevaluate their choice of visuals, whether they're supporting these ideals or not.[6]

Milka has introduced a Beeping Bunny product that provides sonic cues to enable visually impaired young children to participate in Easter egg hunts. The campaign demonstrates an effective way of prioritising inclusivity, going beyond virtue signalling and brand purpose while maintaining sector relevance.[98]

We are living in a melting pot of cultural and racial diversity. There is a significant growth of multiracial relations, which is leading to multiracial, multinational, and therefore multicultural Alpha children. This creates an interesting new multicultural demographic cohort.

Delaying Family Extension Plans

They are more likely to continue the tendency to marry and have children later in life than previous cohorts did. The average age at which the first child is born, according to the Centers for Disease Control and Prevention, will be 30.8 years for women and 33 years for men. In total, due to new breakthroughs in medicine, people gradually begin to live longer.

Interestingly, studies in the field of psychiatry claim that – next to the possible risks of postponing childbirth – children of older parents have a higher IQ, and those with adult mothers have fewer social problems and are more emotionally resilient.

Future studies[6] foresee that Alphas will stay in their parents' home for longer and will not rush to form their own family. Alpha children will probably also need to take more responsibility for their parents and take care of their parents both earlier and longer than we have ever witnessed because of an increase in the average age of becoming parents (referring to paragraph above).

Child Activists & Societal Values

Alpha kids are environmentally savvy, with a clear awareness of global challenges. As they get older, this generation is more interested in brands that truly stand for important values in society. As they grow up, this cohort is increasingly looking for brands with genuine society values.

Alphas advocate for others, themselves and their environment.

(GWI, 2022)[103]

As such Gen Alpha kids are becoming activists even at home, like going on strikes at school or protesting against using things like plastic only once. They don't just accept things without thinking – they question everything, from how people see boys and girls to whether climate change is real. They do what they believe is right.

Children's Courtroom by Counterspace in South Africa is a mobile installation and educational tool for children to learn about the justice system, rights, law and equality.[92]

Gen Alpha children are known for their pestering power. This basically means that they can control or persuade their parents into doing what they want them to do. This could include buying them goods that they might not exactly need. Children believe in two things: persistence and necessity. Their belief in persistence basically states that they won't give up until they get what they want from their parents. They continue nagging until they get what they want, and according to research,[10] parents give in to their children after nine unbearable nagging scenarios.

On the other hand, necessity tends to be more productive than persistence. This involves children engaging in valid arguments with their parents. This strategy is twofold. Either they explain why the thing they want so badly is going to be advantageous for them, or they sum up the disadvantages of their parents' actions when they purchase something for the home, something the children don't want.

But the recent juvenile protests over the environment shows the direction Gen Alpha seems to be heading. One in five of those aged between five and nine have already participated in a march or have protested for something they care about.[10]

Gen Alpha children are significant influencers in their own homes: from the choice of a new family car to next summer's holiday destination to the weekly grocery shopping. They clearly prefer brands that bring purpose and societal value. Gen Alpha children are being guided by their moral compass to focus on 'pestering' for the better.

Gen Alpha and the Pandemic

It has been more than three years since the World Health Organisation declared Covid-19 a pandemic. The pandemic deprived us of many things that we used to do before. Going out was one of those things. People had to stay in and going out was not an option anymore.

Zooming in on Screen Time

Screen time for primary school children increased significantly during the Covid-19 pandemic. A global research review found that these children were spending an extra hour and 20 minutes per day on screens. Initially, all types of media saw a boost during lockdowns, but traditional offline options like newspapers and TV are now returning to their usual trends. However, online TV and music streaming experienced the highest surges, largely due to older people using these services for the first time.

In 2022, subscription-based businesses faced challenges as new competitors entered the market, and people became more mindful of their expenses. In the US, the perception that online TV subscriptions were expensive grew by 27% since the second quarter of 2020, but the intention to cancel such subscriptions decreased by 8%.

The age group most affected by increased screen time was children between six and ten years old. The research also showed that extended screen time negatively impacted both children and adults. This included effects on diet, eye health, mental wellbeing (like anxiety, depression, and loneliness), and overall health (fatigue, reduced physical activity, and weight gain).

During the Covid-19 pandemic's early stages in March to April 2020, there were significant concerns about the future. Although worries about the virus decreased over time, people adapted to the changes in their lives. The pandemic had deep effects on finances, the environment, and people's understanding of what truly matters.

The rise in screen usage had adverse effects on health. It led to poor diets, eye health, and mental wellbeing in children. It also caused behavioural issues like aggression and irritability. This situation prompted calls to address the negative impact on children's health.

Lockdown measures made children rely more on technology for learning and staying connected, but not all children had the skills or resources to stay safe online, which put them at risk for exploitation and mental health problems. For example, Delete-It, a counselling service for children exposed to digital abuse, experienced a 179% increase in queries from 2019 to 2021.

TikTok is introducing a 60-minute usage restriction for users under the age of 18, a move aimed at addressing worries surrounding its addictive influence on teenagers. As concerns over managing screen time continue to rise, there's a growing expectation among parents that social media platforms should take on more responsibility in this regard.[100]

Researchers found that increased screen time, particularly from TV and computers, had negative effects on diet, sleep, mental health, and eye health. Primary school children experienced the largest increase of 83 minutes per day, followed by adults with 58 minutes and adolescents with 55 minutes. Even children under five had a noticeable increase of 35 minutes.

In the UK, like in many countries, school closures due to the pandemic led to on-line classes, affecting students' mental health and wellbeing. Teachers observed reduced resilience, confidence, and increased anxiety among students. The pandemic also influenced subject choices for exams, with fewer students opting for sciences and languages due to confidence issues. Additionally, students' technology skills were impacted, as some were only comfortable with touch-screen devices, neglecting desktops.

A Childwise report states that toddlers are very comfortable with using touch screen devices and take full control of the technology. The most recent survey conveyed by a UK research agency reported the same results stated above. The researchers noticed that compared to 2021 there is a visible increase in screen usage of toddlers (see the table below).

ACTIVITY	2021 (%)	2022 (%)
Can open apps independently	34	42
Can navigate through apps	25	28
Mastering other basic functions	26	42
Watch videos	63	73
Play games	52	56
Educational content	35	41
Draw/colour	34	36
Can record Videos	-	34
Can click pictures	-	32
Can unlock the device if it has a passcode	-	27

Table: Toddlers' Screentime Usage

School going kids and preschoolers mostly use tablets (65%) followed by cell phones (45%) and laptops (20%). Their screen usage time has also increased from 8.8 hours per week in 2021 to 10 hours per week in 2022.[13]

The big picture clearly shows that we should use screens less to avoid problems. These problems include bad eating habits, sleep issues, mental health problems, and eye health troubles. Daniel P. Keating looked at how much time people spent on screens before and during the pandemic. The author studied more than 200,000 people and found out that the pandemic affected people's health differently, just like money does. Even though people had to stay home, some still went outside to exercise by biking or running. This shows how the pandemic affected everyone in various ways.

Media also made people more scared of social media with headlines like 'Have Smartphones Destroyed a Generation?' People worried a lot about young people's mental health and blamed screens, even though there wasn't enough proof. This is like how people used to worry about young people in the past.There are real worries about digital media, especially social media. People are studying this more carefully, including a recently published handbook. Researchers have trouble because social media companies keep their methods secret. They don't let independent researchers study how social media affects young people's confidence and anxiety.

Studies often warn against Alphas' tech addiction, but from an evolutionary perspective, it seems likely that these children will outgrow this 'addiction' faster while mastering digital skills with ease. They will most likely become better users of technology in the long run.

> 'Much of the discussion is framed around fighting "addiction" to technology. But to me, that resembles a moral panic, giving voice to scary claims based on weak data.'
>
> Christopher J. Ferguson,
> Professor of Psychology Stetson University

Other Pandemic Effects on Kids

Alphas, which is the name for the generation affected by Covid-19, are the ones impacted the most. Very young kids, like toddlers and preschoolers, are having a hard time with basic things like writing and talking because of the Covid-19 situation. Researchers are looking into how the pandemic is affecting babies, but it's too early to fully understand the effects. The studies done so far might not be accurate because the parents who joined the studies might be worried about their kids already. Also, wearing face masks during the studies could affect the results a bit.

Some doctors did tests where they asked parents questions, and they found out that babies born during the pandemic scored lower on tests of skills like moving, talking, and using their hands compared to babies born before the pandemic. It didn't matter if the parents had the virus or not; something about the pandemic time itself seemed to affect the babies. Even though most kids are okay if they get Covid-19, early research shows that stress during pregnancy because of the pandemic might harm babies' brains. Parents and caregivers might be acting differently with kids, which could affect how well kids can move and think. The longer the pandemic goes on, the more problems kids seem to have. The issue is that they're not interacting with people as much.

For school-age kids, when they went back to school after the pandemic, some teachers noticed that kids had trouble with talking and understanding language. Babies also had problems with reading people's expressions, maybe because they didn't spend as much time with others due to the pandemic.

Some kids had a hard time with group activities, while very young kids struggled to learn how to share and take turns. Babies might be learning to move less because they aren't playing with friends or going to playgrounds. Research shows that not being around other kids might be slowing some kids down. Older Alphas, the older part of the generation, had trouble with math, reading, and writing. But teachers said that compared to before, these problems were getting better.

Covid-19 was tough for many, but not everyone. Some kids did better because they didn't have to do as much stuff. But for those stuck in homes with problems and no school or activities, it was hard. Some kids got scared to leave their homes even after things got better. They stayed inside more and used screens to avoid problems outside.

The world is getting better in some ways, like how we treat different families and people, but kids still need their parents. Losing a parent can be really hard for a child. When parents fight a lot, it's also tough for kids. Some parents struggle to discipline without being mean, and that's hard for kids and parents. Many things in today's world can bother kids, but there are many positives too.

Masked Effects

Kids who went to school or other places with groups of people during the pandemic often saw others wearing face masks. A big question is whether these masks, which cover parts of the face used for showing feelings and talking, might be affecting how kids learn emotions and talk.

There's a well-known experiment called the 'Still Face' experiment by Tronick (1975). In this experiment, parents talk to their kids without showing any facial expressions. They keep their faces still, which is why it's called 'Still Face'. The results showed that kids first tried to get their parents' attention, but then they felt sad and worried when their parents didn't show any feelings. Tronick got emails from parents who were worried about how masks during the pandemic were affecting their kids. This made Tronick wonder if masks acted like a still face. He asked parents to record videos of them and their babies before, during, and after they put on masks. Babies noticed when parents put on masks – they would change their expressions, look away, or point at the mask – but then they kept playing with their parents like before. Tronick says that masks block just one way of talking. Parents wearing masks still show that they care and want to talk to their kids. The results showed that masks don't really get in the way of understanding feelings or words. Another study in May found that two-year-olds could still understand words even if adults wore masks that covered their faces.

Kids try really hard to be happy and deal with tough situations better than grown-ups. When they're feeling down, they might not show it directly. They might show it in how they act, but it's not easy for parents, teachers, or others to see. Kids can also catch up after hard times when things get better. Most kids will probably be okay in the end, but more kids might be having a tough time now. If we want to help those who are struggling, it's best to help them soon.

Protecting Our Kids

Graham Music, a therapist from Britain who wrote the book 'Nurturing Natures', talks about how kids develop ways to protect themselves when things are hard. A survey in 2021 found that all the kids asked said that the pandemic is still affecting their education. The pandemic has also made the worldwide economy worse, which means about 1.1 billion Alphas are now living in poor conditions.

During the last two years of the pandemic, more kids have become poor. This means they don't have enough for things like school, health, a good place to live, food, and clean water. An organisation called 'Save the Children' got a huge increase in calls from March to April 2021 in India. The helpline got 10 calls in March and 723 calls in April when the number of Covid-19 cases in India went really high. This helpline was started by the State Child Rights Commission and Save the Children to help kids in five places in Rajasthan. The kids who called were from preschool, primary school, and high school.

In South Africa, more than 350 kids were killed in the last three months of 2021. The number of attempted murders went up by 30%, and most of the violence happened at home. In Denmark, a service called Delete-It, which helps kids who face online abuse, got 179% more messages in 2021 compared to 2019. They got 707 messages in 2019 and 1,974 in 2021.

As we think about life after the Covid-19 pandemic, many adults and kids will find it tough to leave behind the fear and uncertainty that came with it. There will be big worries about moving forward. Parents have a tough choice. They want to help their kids by taking away things like social media that can make them anxious and sad. But doing that might make kids feel alone. It seems like a good idea to get rid of phones and social media because they might be causing problems. But there's a problem with just doing that. We're not spending enough time and effort on finding out the real reasons why young people are feeling more anxious and sad.

If we step back and look at things closely, we see that the real issue is the stress that's affecting everyone. This is especially bad for teenagers who are going through a sensitive time in their lives. There's proof that from teenage years to early adulthood, traditional mental health problems happen because of stress. Usually, we focus on the part where some young people have a hard time dealing with stress. But now, many teenagers, even the ones who are generally okay, are just overwhelmed by too much stress. Building resilience, which means helping them handle problems better, is important, but we shouldn't forget that stress is a big part of the problem.

The real reasons behind this big stress lie in our society. It would be a mistake for psychologists to only look at things like how teenagers deal with stress and become stronger. Telling them to be stronger and handle stress better can't solve everything, especially when there are so many different stresses all around us. A few triggers might be: the problems with the environment, the increase in racism, treating women badly, white supremacy, and laws against LGBTQ people; the political changes that take away rights like choosing whether to have a baby or voting, with more changes on the way, like laws against same-sex marriage and relationships; lots of gun violence, making safe places like schools, churches, and public events scary; more differences in money, wealth, and health during development, and more pressure to compete to have a good position in society.

Meditation app Calm has added Disney-related content to tackle back-to-school anxiety in kids. Amid a growing mental health crisis among Gen Alphas and tweens, parents and kids are looking to brands to introduce kids to mindfulness and meditation to promote lifelong practices and wellbeing.[97]

Alphas and Their Purchasing Power

The young generation is commonly known for their strong beliefs and values that guide them about what to buy and who to buy it from. As mentioned before, this generation already has spending power and can make their own purchasing decisions. The technology has made them able to follow the trends and decide what they want to buy using their thoughtful buying ability guided by strong ethical values i.e. their support for green movement, diversity and inclusion, and standing for what is right.

An example of this is the sustainable soap company Gelo who invented the 'Parent Track' that children can install on their parents' devices. It uses 'ad tracking in a way that persistently reminds parents, wherever they go across the web or their devices to shop sustainably.'[95]

With fast and constant wireless internet, this generation has learned, entertained, and distracted themselves using shiny screens made of glass, plastic, and metal. They're also familiar with how apps make money, like buying things inside apps, subscriptions, small payments, and paying to win in games. This new way of using mobile devices will even change how they shop, and they might even ask their parents to download more apps.

More than half of the surveyed Alphas mentioned that they would like to buy things if their favourite YouTube or Instagram personality uses, wears, or enjoys those items. Influencers have become even more important than family members when it comes to influencing the buying choices of children. Around 14% of Alphas are interested in the idea of influencers having their own stores. When it comes to influencing children, online videos are the most effective channels.

This shifts the influencers' roles to retailers and not just partners or ambassadors. Once the influencers have captured Alphas' attention, the product will inevitably go viral and sell in no time. That is why it is about time that brands start investing in social media commerce and Gen Z or Alpha influencers.

The differences in preferences, which are influenced by gender and where they live, show that decisions about what kind of content, media, and channels to use cannot be the same for every member of this generation. Instead, these choices need to be made more carefully for different groups within this generation. They receive a lot of messages from brands. Without changing how things are done, retailers won't be able to effectively use influencers to turn Alphas into customers. About 41% of kids tag their friends on Instagram when they see something they might want to buy. This is most common among teenagers.

Parents, influenced by their children, are also actively considering saving as a serious matter. This suggests that despite having purchasing power at this young age, Gen Alpha are not irrational spenders, they are spending only on the things that they think are worth their attention and money. They are mature enough to save and invest their money thus teaching their elders the importance of the two.[19]

Gen Alpha has significant spending power and is showing a particular preference for certain brands that use innovative technology to create successful marketing efforts aimed at the young generation. For example, McDonald's has partnered with Snapchat to create filters and games that are specifically designed for younger users. This has helped to engage Gen Alpha in a unique way, and it has made the brand more appealing to them.

Gen Alpha parents are also increasingly turning to their children for advice on where to eat and what to buy. This means that Gen Alpha is likely to have a significant impact on the food and beverage industry in the coming years. This makes Gen Alpha a highly influential consumer group.[20]

Branding & Consumerism to Alphas

From a very young age, Alpha children start knowing about the notion of brands and even forming connections with the brands they like. A lot of kids have heard about Amazon, and 72% of them like the company. Among 13- to 16-year-olds, 90% know about Amazon, for 10- to 12-year-olds, it's 88%, while 74% of 6- to 9-year-olds know about it. This means that Amazon is really good at catching the attention of Alphas. Surprisingly, more kids know about Amazon than they do about Apple and Nike, which are two of the biggest and most well-known brands in the world. When asked what Amazon is famous for, 62% said shopping, 17% said fast delivery, 6% said voice assistants, and 5% said TV shows and movies.

Only 39% of kids trust Alexa, and 43% are not sure if they trust it. About a quarter of kids have used Alexa or another voice assistant to buy things online, and 41% of kids plan to shop using Alexa when they grow up.

Looking at online shopping, 55% prefer to buy or download things online. Most of Generation Alpha likes going to real shops, and 47% enjoy shopping on the main shopping streets. Only 38% like buying things online instead of going to a physical store. From these numbers, it seems that focusing only on digital shopping could make many future shoppers unhappy, as a lot of them still like real stores and the whole shopping experience. In fact, kids want both the physical store and the online store to be similar, with 74% saying they like seeing the same things in shops and online. This creates an opportunity of 'branding'.

Are Alphas Susceptible to Branding?

While being heavily influenced by brands and branding, Alphas' ability to understand and decipher the real purpose of branding is still developing. There is concern that this renders them more likely to believe what advertisers tell them. The social influence of branding can cause tension in family households, especially if the trendy brand in question happens to be twice as expensive as most other brands in the same product range. Brands use the promise of instant social status. If brands form part of early consumer socialisation which enhances the consumer literacy of children in terms of their abilities to identify quality and value in commodities and services, this could actually be seen as a positive outcome. An unhealthy obsession with brands can be created where premium brands drive younger consumers' commodity preferences with essential items such as food and clothing.

Understanding Early Consumer Development: Model 1

To understand how children learn about consumerism, we need to consult models of child development. They describe processes or stages of development that provide an essential underpinning to how children learn and are able to comprehend what is going on around them in their environment. A great deal of marketing research and theorising about how children learn to become consumers has been shaped by Piaget's model. Piaget proposed that there are four key stages of cognitive development that shape the way kids think about the world around them. The first one is the **sensorimotor stage** (from birth to 2 years). Kids learn how to interpret basic sensations from the world around them and how to control and perform their physical movements. Their language and underlying cognitive abilities are limited. Understanding brand and related marketing messages tend to be beyond their capabilities. Then we have the **preoperational stage** (2–7 years). Kids begin to acquire language skills, they can verbally label objects and communicate internal thoughts and feelings to others. In this stage, they retain a highly egocentric view of the world despite entering into a broader range of social interactions and relationships with others. Kids at this age have difficulty in dealing with more than one variable at a time when making a judgment about objects. This explains their limited understanding of advertising. In the **concrete operational stage** (7–11 years), kids learn to retain and reproduce ideas about objects and processes without always needing those things to be physically present and visible. At this age children could still experience difficulty with their interpretation of some promotional messages about brands because of their ephemeral nature. But they might also begin to make their own judgments about products linked to brands if they can physically experience the products. The last stage is the **formal operational stage** (11– adulthood). Children learn to think analytically and in far more abstract ways. They become aware of the need to weigh up the implications of actions not only for themselves but for others.

At this point, they can think about brands not just based on what they personally like or don't like, but they can also understand how other people, especially their friends, might feel about a brand. They might even choose a brand based on what their group likes, even if they personally prefer something else. Later theories about how the mind grows and learns shifted away from what Piaget believed.

Understanding Early Consumer Development: Model 2

Another model to understand how children become informed and selective consumers is from Deborah Roedder John. She developed a model that conformed with the idea that kids go through several stages of cognitive and social development. Within each of these stages they develop their ability to recognise that advertising is something distinctive and the ability to make sense of it. A newer model challenges the position adopted by this cognitive defence perspective and recognises that sometimes, especially when consumers become emotionally involved with advertisements, young consumers fail to implement their learned defences against persuasion. Deborah Roedder John outlined three categories of information processing relating to the study of children's socialisation as consumers. These are called strategic processors, cued processors and limited processors. Her initial thinking about an information processing approach to the assessment of children's abilities as young consumers had begun twenty years earlier. Information processing theories have underpinned studies that have investigated how children learn to pay attention to the world around them and then select which of their experiences they will process and store information about for later use. These theories also address how children organise this internalised information – or knowledge – and are then able to retrieve and use it later.[21]

Reaching Alphas Through Digital Advertising

Marketers are interested in using digital media to reach Alphas because many kids use these communication platforms a lot. All around the world, it's clear that those under 18 years old use digital media more than any other age group. Kids from wealthier families with more money tend to use the internet more. Social media websites have also become a big part of how children make friends. Brand marketing has had to adapt to this new promotional environment because consumers engage with it differently from traditional mass media. There are other marketing techniques that have opened up through the internet, which entail the recruitment of consumers to act as endorsers of a brand to their friends and other people they know.

Interactivity of the Digital World

The digital world provides a platform on which consumers can be engaged with brands in a more dynamic way than through traditional mass media. This is something that has excited brand marketers.

Brand marketers use different online tools to connect with people. They have websites for their brands where people can visit. There are also online communities where people can talk to each other about things they like. You can find websites where you can 'shop' online and then get the things in real life. There are ads that pop up on the screen, banners with info, emails, and newsletters that tell you about deals and promotions. When these online tools let people interact, it makes them feel like they're in control of learning about the brand. It makes them want to know more.

Also many virtual worlds targeting children have been launched. On these sites kids can link with other users, as they can through standard online social networks, but they can also wander a virtual world in the form of an avatar. There are several sites such as Edmodo, Gant Hello, Togetherville, and What's What, that look a lot like Facebook. One of the most popular sites dedicated to children is Yoursphere, which takes members aged under 18. Kids can link with each other, start a blog or join virtual groups in multiplayer games.

A great brand example that successfully targeted Gen Alpha is Lego – more specifically with their Lego Life campaign. Lego Life is an app, actually a safe social media platform for kids to share their latest Lego creations and to connect online with their friends, other parents and young Lego enthusiasts. This in turn created a sense of community. *'What made this campaign successful was its emphasis on the environment, safety, and community building,'* according to Narciso from Dubitify.[94]

Lego Life App – which is a safe social media platform for parents & kids!

Web Advertising

Using websites to advertise brands has raised worries, especially when they're aimed at kids. Studies show that children start noticing ads and can tell they're different, but just being able to make basic comparisons doesn't mean young children fully get how ads work and why they're trying to persuade them.

However, high usage of social media, pressure imposed by peers and advertising is harmfully influencing young minds. In her blog on thred.com, Sofia Phillips[22] discussed a campaign by Dove (a popular beauty brand) in which they studied the effects of beauty standards on the mental health of kids. The purpose of the campaign was to study and raise awareness about the negative impacts of societal pressures of beauty standards on young minds and their wellbeing. The survey was conducted on youngsters aged 11–17 years old. Results revealed that they feel the need to meet unreal beauty standards imposed by society. Constant exposure to edited, filtered images can lead to mental health issues as well as low self-esteem, anxiety and depression.

The campaign aimed to promote a more diverse and inclusive definition of beauty and challenged these false beauty standards. They encouraged the youth to embrace their individualities and unique qualities thus building their self-esteem, building a positive body image and improving their mental wellbeing.

Brand Engagement Through Social Media

The nature of young consumer engagement via online social media invokes a different approach to branding in which the consumer is 'empowered' to contribute to brand design and promotion. Does this approach disguise marketing activity to the extent that children are less likely to become aware of what is happening than they would in the case of more transparent branding activities, even when they have reached a more advanced stage of cognitive development? Children cannot be conceived as a single homogenous consumer category. They use social media to keep in touch with friends, but it can be dangerous if they share too much personal information on these platforms. Kids often don't see the problem; social media use is the norm among them. Despite Facebook's age limit (at least 13) a lot of Alphas are also already active on this platform.

Advergames

Another way of digital branding is through advergames. Advergames are electronic games children are invited to play that contain a product or brand. Advergames can provide important features: the degree of integration between the brand and game; viral marketing invitations to players to send emails to friends to encourage them to play; allowing players to customise specific aspects of games to make them personally more relevant. Advergames tend to have a short playing time and therefore do not demand a lot of the player's time. Furthermore, the disguised nature of brand advertising in this setting might also mean a lower risk of rejection by young consumers. This disguised nature of brand promotions in advergames is one of the public concerns.

Advergames Are Better Than Banner Advertisements

Banner advertising has been found to have questionable effectiveness. Click-through rates have been consistently registered as very low. A standalone message on the website is not really effective. Advertisements that have animated elements and interactive components proved to be twice as effective as banner advertisements. A positive outcome for the brand image is enhanced when a brand is thematically related to games content.

What's Next?
Alphas and Career Development

What about Alphas' future jobs? Many of them are passionate about environmental careers. Around 67% of 6–9-year-olds want to focus on saving the planet when they grow up. In the United States, 66% of kids feel this way, and in the UK, it's 60%. It's not surprising that they want to support businesses that match their values and take care of the environment and society.

While there are many resources available for adults to help with career planning, there is a lack of similar resources for children. By introducing career development content to kids at a young age, they can be better prepared to make informed decisions about their future. This can help to increase their chances of success in the workforce and improve their overall quality of life.

One way to introduce career development content to kids is through educational programming. By creating shows that feature different professions and career paths, children can learn about different job opportunities and what it takes to succeed in those fields. For example, a show could follow a veterinarian as they care for animals, giving kids an inside look at what the job entails.

In addition to educational programming, other interactive content could allow kids to explore different careers. This might include virtual reality experiences that simulate a day in the life of someone in a particular profession or gamified apps that help kids identify their strengths and interests and suggest potential career paths.

Another approach to creating career development content for kids is through partnerships with businesses and organisations. By working with companies in different industries, creators can provide kids with access to experts who can share their experiences and provide guidance on how to enter those fields. This could include virtual job shadowing experiences or mentorship programmes that connect kids with professionals in their area of interest.

There are several challenges to creating career development content for kids, including ensuring that the content is age-appropriate and engaging, addressing diversity and inclusion in career representation, and navigating potential ethical concerns, such as promoting certain professions over others.

However, by addressing these challenges and creating high-quality career development content for kids, creators and educators can help prepare the next generation for success in the workforce. This can also help to promote social mobility and reduce economic inequality by providing children with the tools and resources they need to succeed regardless of their background.

Bharanidharan[23] highlights the importance of introducing career development content to kids at a young age and suggests several ways in which this can be done. While there are challenges to creating this type of content, the potential benefits are significant, both for individuals and for society as a whole.

What's Next?
Alphas' role in Climate Change and Climate Rights

Climate rights refer to the idea that future generations have the right to live in a world that is not threatened by the impacts of climate change, such as extreme weather events, rising sea levels, and food and water scarcity.

Jocelyn Timperley has outlined the urgency of the climate crisis and the devastating impacts it is already having on the planet. She declared that the current generation has a responsibility to take action to address the crisis, but that this is not enough on its own. Future generations must also be taken into account, and that should have a say in the decisions that are being made today.

She also explored the concept of intergenerational justice, which refers to the idea that each generation has a responsibility to ensure that future generations are not unfairly burdened by the actions of the past. This concept is based on the idea that we have a moral obligation to leave the world in a better state than we found it, and that this obligation extends to future generations.

There are several challenges to implementing climate rights. One of the key challenges is the fact that climate change is a global problem that requires co-ordinated action on an international scale. This means that it can be difficult to ensure that the needs and rights of future generations are taken into account in decision-making processes.

There are several potential solutions to the challenge of ensuring climate rights. One of them is to incorporate the concept of climate rights into national and international laws and policies. This could involve creating legal frameworks that ensure that the interests of future generations are taken into account in decision-making processes.[24]

Technology could also play an important role in ensuring climate rights. Advances in technology could help to mitigate the impacts of climate change and create a more sustainable future for future generations. However, technology is not a panacea and it must be developed and implemented in a way that takes into account the interests of future generations.

We have a moral obligation to ensure that future generations have the right to a stable climate, and we must take action now to ensure that this right is protected.

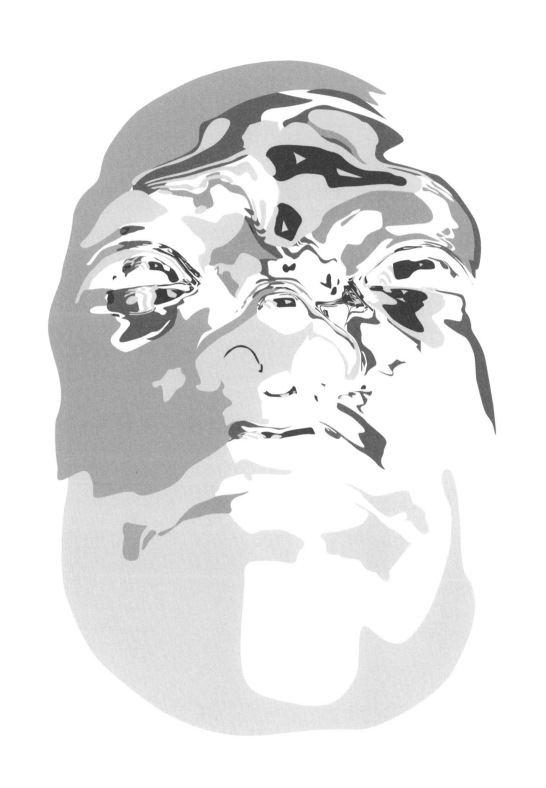

Chapter 4:
Characteristics of Gen Z

Who Are They?

Generation Z, also known as Gen Z or Post Millennials, is a 'force' driving their own lives. Globally forming 34% of the total population, they are regarded as the 'most' generation because of their characteristics, being the most racially and ethnically diverse, most tech savvy, most educated and most globally intelligent generation so far. They couldn't care less about labels, and only believe in YOLO (you only live once). Gen Z openly confirms non-binary ideas of gender and sexuality. They have also redefined other ideas of life like healthcare, branding, marketing, workplace, economy, politics. They are the toughest generation considering what they have seen in their short lives so far i.e. the economic changes, the pandemic, the lockdown drills and much more. Going through this much trauma, now they have nothing to lose which makes them the greatest generation of the 21st century.

For a better understanding, we researched this generation and finally we were able to understand what makes Gen Z 'The Gen Z'.

'Redefining gender roles and finding oneself,
they are living lives on their own terms.'

Key Values

Gen Z have high spirituality but are not religious in nature, realists yet optimistic, they are redefining life in all aspects including gender roles and politics. Traditional factors like age and gender do not play much role in this generation's lives. They believe in elements like family (50%), personality (63%), hobbies (48%), and moral values (47%). This generation is on a journey to find their inner-selves. They are a creative bunch of youngsters (34% creativity) with good humour (34%) and open-minded personalities (30%). They believe in diversity and inclusion and want the brands to understand their priorities. They are also changing the workplace to a more comfortable, understanding, and discrimination-free environment where everyone respects each other's choice of gender norms or beauty standards.

Gen Z's are realists who see the world through glasses of realism yet are still very optimistic. The change in economic conditions and a pandemic followed by a great recession has made them even more sensitive. They spend less on luxury items like cars or bigger homes. It has also made them lose faith in traditional 9–5 jobs. They are tending towards online work and work from home because the pandemic made the unemployment rate among Gen Z the highest by the end of 2020.

Choosing Their Own Career Paths

Despite all these problems, Gen Zers kept their cool and stayed optimistic. Even though they are under pressure to be productive they do not follow older generations; rather they choose their own paths. Their situation made them convinced that in order to succeed in life they should not adopt traditional paths to success but they needed to create new ways. We for example see how Gen Z is seeking employment through expressive short videos – 'TikTok Resumes'.

Seven out of ten Gen Zers believe that they can change society. Research from Reuters Institute Oxford suggests that Gen Z are optimistic, seek non-traditional ways to succeed, are comfortable with taking risks and redefining career paths. There is 53% more probability of them taking an unconventional career path and they are 57% more likely to bend working rules. They not only believe in YOLO but are firm believers of YDY (you do you).

Desire to Redefine Traditional Standards

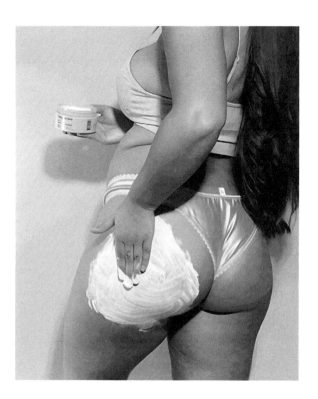

They are practically raised on social media and are very comfortable with their media-friendly marketable personalities but 17% less likely to be content with their looks. Unlike the earlier generations, instead of fixing their looks, Gen Z focus on fixing beauty standards. They hate heavily photoshopped images on social media and expect beauty brands to disclose if images used by them have any photoshop or airbrushing. They are more likely to associate themselves with brands that use genuine/raw photos and real skin in their marketing campaigns. Beauty brand Megababe for example is very popular with Gen Z: they promote solutions for beauty problems we don't talk about (enough). Think for example of creams for a sweaty butt, chafing thighs etc.

Superfluid

Also skincare brand Superfluid is a hit amongst them as they show real imagery of real people with real skin and real stories – through user-generated content.

In the UK, one out of five Gen Zers today identify as non hetero-sexual. From fashion to sexuality, this generation hates being labelled and embraces inclusivity. They are more at ease in wearing gender neutral clothes. As compared to other generations, Gen Z is 75% more comfortable in wearing opposite gender or gender neutral clothing.

Even though they believe in a higher power, they are not religious. According to the research mentioned in the image, 24% of Gen Zers in the US are less likely to associate themselves with a religion (Christianity, Islam, Judaism, and other religions), while in the UK Gen Z is 13% less likely (in comparison with other generations) to associate with any religion. But even though they do not associate with any religion, they still believe in a higher power and practise manifesting, positive affirmations and other spiritual virtues.

More Characteristics

Some other characteristics of Gen Z described by Buller and fellows[1] are described as below:

Social consciousness: Gen Z is aware of the impact of climate change and is more likely to take action to address it, such as donating money, volunteering, or protesting. Beauty brand Rare Beauty, which has a clear purpose, is an example of a brand that Gen Z would follow for these reasons.

Pragmatism: They are known for their practicality and are expected to demand even more from their employers than previous generations.

Diversity: Gen Z is highly diverse and expect to express their worldview and express their expectations of inclusivity and diversity in all aspects of life.

Technologically savvy: They are comfortable using technology from a very young age and are expected to have fluid career paths, with many of the jobs they will hold in the future not yet existing.

Cross-generational education: There is a growing interest in cross-generational education, with older people learning from the social consciousness of Gen Z.

Post-patronising: Brands can collaborate and work with this generation to inspire older people to engage in the topics they care about, such as green education, inclusion, anti-racism movements etc ...

Pocket money economy: Gen Z is taking control of their finances and wising up to positive money habits, even learning about money in gaming spaces.[25]

Entrepreneurial streak: They are compelled to invest in non-traditional channels and are already owning cryptocurrency and making and selling things on the internet.[25]

> 'According to the Spotify 2023 Culture Next Report US 42% of GenZ listeners have listened to podcast in faster speed and 66% have listened to sped up songs.'

Where Are They?

Older generations used to rely on mainstream media for news, entertainment and other information. In previous eras, the flow of information was scheduled and people used to receive it from certain trusted sources like TV channels, newspapers, magazines or radio. But nowadays the flow of information has accelerated. You can find any piece of information online in a matter of seconds. It is the era of social media platforms like YouTube, Instagram, TikTok, Snapchat and ByteDance (a Chinese short-video platform which got popular in the US and the UK during Covid lockdown in 2020) where it takes only a few minutes for any piece of information to go viral. Gen Zers rely on social media for any kind of news. They do not go and confirm it through news channels. On these platforms, the algorithm shows media according to viewer's choice. It learns the user's scrolling patterns i.e. which type of content caught their attention and where they hovered longer, then it shows more content like that. This way the users can control the kind of information that they want to see or not want to see.

> 'Everybody knows that the media has been exposed so many times over and over again of them lying to us. And I think that they're taking advantage of our ignorance. All media is somewhat owned by a bigger corporation that just gets bigger and bigger. If all these people at the top are friends, it makes you think they're trying to control what you see.'
>
> 23, transitioning to med school,
> she/her, New York

But, in using social media as the basic source of information, there are many risks involved. These platforms have a lot of fake news and misinformation. Even though Gen Z have ways to fact check information, it does not make them immune to wrong information. 60% of Gen Zers think that short videos and short articles (in spite of being their favourite mode of content delivery) do not provide the full picture of the story and they might fall for misinformation. Almost the same proportion of youngsters said that they have developed techniques to filter fake news. The research also shows that compared to older generations, Gen Z is far less concerned about the damage done by misinformation because for this generation, the benefits of social media outweigh its drawbacks.

Research shows that when Gen Z wants to search for something, they do not use any search engine. They go and search it on TikTok. This piece of information is very useful for the brands and marketers, if they want to target Gen Z. The brands and marketers need to work with the Gen Z influencers/creators because this generation does not like to get information by experts or representatives from companies, rather they trust influencers and social media creators of their own age. They trust content on TikTok because it's raw and made by people their own age to whom they can relate. They use TikTok as a source of news. They find the app to be trustworthy and an accessible platform for news. Since Gen Z appreciates short but engaging videos, they like to use TikTok for its content. They also think it is reliable because the content shared on TikTok is created by common people who are neither celebrities nor TV producers/directors. Gen Z's preference for TikTok reflects their inclination towards digital media and platforms that align with their interests and habits.[25] That is why, to get their attention, brands and marketers need to create raw and relatable content. For Gen Z, it is not just 'what' is being delivered and by 'whom' but the 'how it is being delivered' which matters a great deal. Dutch NOS Stories and the Belgian @nws.nws.nws therefore are a hit with Gen Z because their snackable & easy-to-digest video news formats on TikTok and Instagram provide them with all the updates in an instant & human way. Another example that lives amongst Gen Z is 'Too Long, Don't Read' which is a 1-minute newsletter with the key headlines.

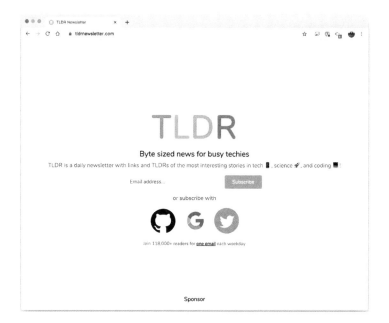

How Gen Z Feels

Gen Z has been through a lot including terrorism, economic and environmental changes, pandemic, lockdown and climate change. All of these situations have added to the stress which makes this generation more focused on wellbeing both physical and mental.

These are all US-based headlines that have shaped Gen Z's common personality traits: experiences such as George Floyd's murder, the climate crisis, the pandemic, remote learning, Australian wildfires, love life being distanced and delayed, the QAnon storm of the Capitol.

This wellbeing is not limited to mental or physical health only, as typical of Gen Z, they have redefined the boundaries of healthcare as well. This generation talks about the issues that were considered embarrassing and private before like acne or irritable bowel syndrome. Gen Z has shone light on all types of health related issues that were never discussed before including female health issues like menstruation, PCOS/PCOD, and fertility.

Compared to older generations, Gen Z are more likely to admit that they are going through a tough phase of life and they need help to cope with the situation. Almost half of Gen Z says that they are going through therapy or being treated for stress, anxiety, depression, or other mental health conditions. One of the reasons might be the pressure they have inflicted upon themselves. They feel responsible for the actions of prior generations and they feel empathetic towards others. One other reason might be the comparisons made on social media which can lead to a feeling of dissatisfaction.

'The most recent 2023 study from dcdx, "From Digital Natives to Digital Captives", asked, "If you could change one thing about social media, what would it be?" 47% of Gen Z said they'd make it easier to disconnect.'

As much as the pandemic is the reason behind this surge of mental health conditions, a documented rise in mental health struggles and celebrities openly talking about it can also be among the major reasons. This generation is also open minded and does not completely rely on medical treatments, rather they experiment and try other treatments like botanical medicine or energy healing. While older generations completely turned towards medical professionals for any illness, only about half of this generation does, which might be a concern for the medical professionals in the future. Good healthcare must have these three things in order to get attention from Gen Z:

1. **Good Vibes**
   Healthcare should feel good. It needs to be inclusive, affirmative, soothing and nurturing. They prefer healthcare that feels like visiting a spa.
2. **Facts**
   Along with good vibes, the healthcare must also be backed by some good research and scientific evidence.
3. **The Option to slide into Direct Messages**
   Gen Z prefer their doctors and nurses to be available online, so they can message anytime and ask about their problems.

Sofia Phillips[26] talks about a phenomenon called 'compassion fatigue'; she says that there exists a feeling of emotional exhaustion and indifference towards others' pain and suffering among the Gen Z. This feeling is caused by being constantly exposed to news and tragic photos on different social media platforms. The overwhelming amount of exposure to tragic news on a daily basis through social media, news websites and other digital platforms has made them numb or insensitive making it challenging to process and empathise with the distress. They may find it difficult to maintain a genuine emotional response to each new tragedy they encounter.

Sofia suggests that limiting the amount of screen time and taking breaks from news updates can affect the mind in a positive way. Gen Z must set boundaries for their mental health and focus on self-care. Engaging in activities that promote self-care and emotional resilience can be beneficial for mental and physical health.

What Gen Z Cares About

There are many young activists from around the world that are protesting against the taboos of older generations, inequality, injustice, war and much more. Youngsters like Malala Yousafzai, Amika George, Greta Thunberg, David Hogg and others show us that Gen Z is in a continuous fight with the status quo. They do not trust their governments like elder generation protestors. The difference between Gen Z and older generations is that this generation does not wait to get to college and then start protesting, rather they start early and that too through online campaigns which makes their reach far more than the previous generations. They are 68% more likely than other generations to engage in issues they care about through social media and are over twice as likely to say it has shaped their beliefs on issues. Where the previous movements needed years to lay the foundation for protest, today's generation can achieve double those results in a half time.

Gen Z believes individual power can bring change. They rely on their employers rather than the government. According to youngsters today, change starts from within and if their workplaces do not agree with their values they usually start looking for other jobs where the employers' values are aligned with theirs. At workplaces which do not 'connect' with the young employees, Gen Zers are more likely to avoid the events or gatherings and be less engaged at work. This generation is always in activist mode and will change their decisions based on their values e.g. if their favourite brands do not care about the global issues that they themselves care about, they will stop buying them.

On one hand this generation talks about wellbeing, talks green, wants to work for green companies, prioritises affordability while purchasing and will buy clothes that are lower in price but on the other hand spends a lot a lot on fashion and clothing despite being financially unstable thus creating a disconnection between their intent and action.

Gen Z don't only 'want' products or workplaces to align with their values but they 'demand' it. Companies need to understand this otherwise they will suffer as this generation becomes financially more powerful. It also creates an opportunity for employers, as Gen Z does not trust their governments, but companies can develop their trust by taking leadership roles in the issues that attract Gen Z the most and which need attention overall as well. They can do it in six ways:

1. Provide more opportunities through social media impact
2. Use social media not only for telling but 'showing' your side of the story
3. Prove your loyalty towards sustainability through your labels and taglines
4. Donate to good causes
5. Hire a dedicated senior executive for sustainability
6. Talk about successes, but even more important, also your failures. Be authentic.

Financial Condition of Gen Z

After seeing their elders struggle financially through tough times like the pandemic and recession afterwards, Gen Z now are not satisfied with their financial condition. Half of Gen Zers are stressed about their financial stability which makes them 1.4 times more likely to report mental stress regarding financial condition.

This generation tries to manage their personal finances through watching tutorials on social media. As mentioned earlier, social media is also a den of misinformation, which is why Gen Zers are anxious and uncertain about what to do or what not to do, but it also fuels their motivation to earn more, thus making them the 'most financially involved' generation so far.

As in every other field of life, this generation is redefining investing as well. Gen Z wants to have fun while making money. They have started investing at an earlier age than the Millennials and that too at a higher rate of return. Usually youngsters today start investing by the age of 21. They are also breaking diversity barriers in investing. Today in the UK Black and Asian representation in investing has increased to 60% while in the USA, it has increased to 1.7x and 1.4x compared to the older generations. Young females today are also investing 1.5x more than the older generations. For investing decisions as well, Gen Z turns to social media. Thirty percent of young investors have invested in the stock recommended on social media like Reddit or TikTok and they have mixed experiences from their investment decisions.

As described by Wyman,[27] Gen Z is in a *'situationship'* with money. They understand that money is a 'necessary evil' without which it is impossible to survive in this world, but they also are of the view that they want to spend money on things that bring them happiness. They are wise enough to know that there are things more important than money but they also prefer security and stability in their personal finance. For the financial companies to get investments from the

Gen Zers it is necessary to respect their values, develop a strong social media game and develop their trust.

How to Target Gen Z Customers

Gen Z, being a tech savvy generation, claims that they can spot fake reviews and other bogus marketing tricks by marketers and brands to attract customers. This generation is a native on social media with larger social media communities that can make any brand a hit or a flop. They also depend on their acquaintances', friends' and family's opinions or recommendations while choosing any brand or a product. According to Wyman, 'They are socially conscious, fiercely independent, highly opinionated, and always connected'. Compared to their predecessors, this generation expects more from brands. Their loyalty towards brands remains as long as the brands show respect for their values. They are a sensitive generation which enjoys a good sense of humour which is not used at the expense of anyone's feelings and is more likely to drop brands if they do so. Gen Z have higher moral values that they prioritise in every way of life. If marketers want to target youngsters today, they should stop treating them just as consumers but recognise that this generation demands to be prioritised. They need relevant content that can be trusted and has no 'red flags'.

'Brand Loyalty' does not go well with this generation. They look for affordable and cheap brands with high quality products. If a brand offers more affordable products, they are more likely to ditch their current favourite and go for the cheaper ones with good quality. The only way to gain their loyalty is to align with their values, call out the issues boldly and opt for sustainability.

Gen Zers' hatred for being labelled or discriminated against makes them redefine the marketing experience. They have all the products at their fingertips and can shop from the comfort of their homes in no time. As described in the previous section, Gen Z is the most financially independent generation so far and they are going to be the largest consumer demographic in history.

This generation's buying habits differ from the previous generations. Gen Z is more opinionated and highly connected with their values. They prefer brands which show more corporate social responsibility, sustainability, inclusivity, authenticity and engagement towards their consumers' values. This is the reason behind their absence of loyalty for a single brand. Youngsters from the USA and UK are more likely to buy from online search (17%) or through social media (24%). Even though they love to shop online, one in 10 Gen Zers miss shopping physically in stores.

Instead of just believing online reviews, Gen Z prefers to buy products recommended by their family and friends. Being social media natives, they crave online communities that speak for important issues and discuss experiences with brands. The marketers now need to consider marketing as an online conversation with their consumers and join the communities created by Gen Zers to know about their preferences.The majority (three-fifths) of youngsters say that it is important for brands to have a social media presence. They can trust the quality of products/services if that brand has social media accounts. Keeping this in mind, the brands and marketers can adopt the following steps for winning them as customers:

• Create online spaces that keep the communication between brands and Gen Zers
• Practise being more authentic
• Build a community where young people can have a sense of belonging
• Accept and appreciate *'phygital'* experience as young people embrace online presence

To grab Gen Z's attention, brands and content creators have to adapt their strategies by focusing on short videos with visually appealing content, shared on a platform heavily used by Gen Z. Brands and marketers also need to care about Gen Z's values if they want to effectively engage with this generation.

Gen Z and The Metaverse

Being digital natives, Gen Zers are likely to be early adopters of the metaverse. Brands should consider leveraging this new platform to engage with this demographic. Hence the metaverse has emerged as a potential space for brands to engage with Gen Z in Europe.

As already mentioned Gen Z have a strong affinity for technology, and according to a recent study, 81% of them have participated in activities related to the metaverse. These activities include playing online games (48%), creating avatars (29%), using virtual reality headsets (20%), watching e-sports

(18%), and visiting branded spaces in games (12%). Despite their familiarity with these activities, Gen Z are not naive and recognise both the positive and negative aspects of the digital world. They believe that everyone is equal in a virtual world (41%) and have online friends they have never met in person (46%). However, they also feel the pressure to present an idealised version of themselves online (48%), and they are concerned about data privacy (50%) and the way social media companies are using their data. Although they maintain many friendships online, Gen Z values in-person interaction, with 54% recognising its importance during the pandemic. They also attempt to limit their smartphone use (36%).

Fashion brands such as Gucci and Louis Vuitton have created virtual fashion shows in the metaverse, while gaming companies such as Epic Games and Ubisoft have partnered with brands such as Nike and Mercedes-Benz to create in-game advertising campaigns. These early experiments are just the tip of the iceberg and many more brands are likely to enter the metaverse in the coming years.

Brands should keep in mind when entering the metaverse the need to create experiences that are authentic, engaging, and relevant to Gen Z, as well as the need to respect the privacy and data rights of users. Brands that are able to navigate these challenges successfully could reap significant rewards in terms of customer engagement, loyalty, and brand equity.[30] More on Gen ZAlphas and the metaverse can be found in Chapter 6.

Snack, the dating app first released in late 2021 with a TikTok-like interface, is bringing AI to the dating scene. The app has introduced an AI feature enabling

Gen Z users to meet in the metaverse using avatars before arranging real-life dates. Users have the ability to generate AI-trained avatars that represent themselves, allowing these virtual personas to navigate Snack's metaverse dating realm and engage in conversations with avatars of other users. Should the avatar detect potential compatibility, it alerts the user, who can then choose whether to initiate a human-to-human conversation at their discretion. This development underscores Gen Z's preference for a more detached approach to counter the anxiety-inducing aspects of dating app dynamics and online interactions.[105]

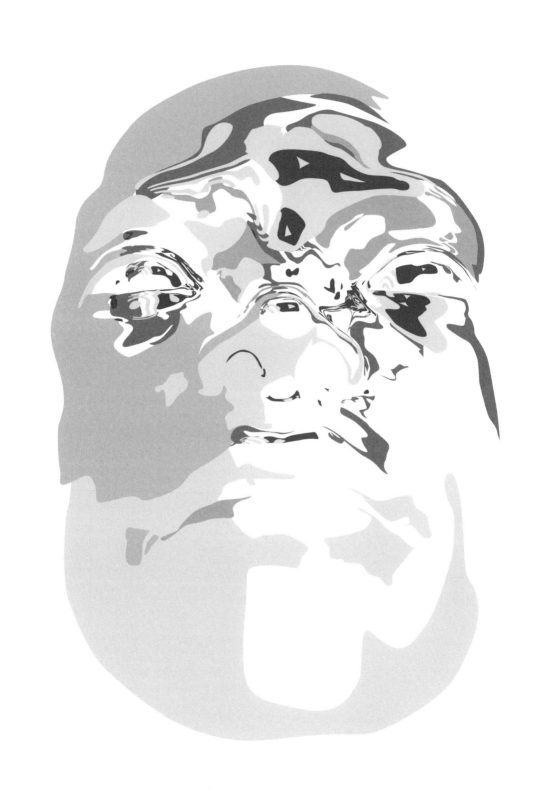

Chapter 5:
ZAlphas' Behaviour Online

'...young people have always been eager to make their mark on the world, so it's really exciting to live in a time when we actually can!'

Alina Morse
Teenpreneur, speaker, inventor, & CEO, Zollicandy

ZAlphas turn their emotions into actions, challenging existing social structures such as entrepreneurship. The world is changing, and it is easy to recognise that there is no optimal age or condition for starting a business. Youngsters, with their natural interest in tech-empowered creativity, seek new monetisation strategies that go beyond outdated systems. An inspiring idea, self-confidence, and indestructible energy are the only guarantees of success.

Having mastered digital skills, Gen ZAlpha enjoys designing, making and building things. They have the potential to become a cohort of creative digital entrepreneurs, valuing the talent and skills of both others and themselves, and having the vision to translate creativity into business realities.

Kid influencers, or 'kidfluencers', have taken over the internet and seem to control it better than we do, giving them much fame and popularity. These kidfluencers are remodelling online advertising. According to research by Mediakix, companies will generally spend roughly between five and ten billion dollars to pay these influencers for sponsored work in the next few years. Popular brands across the world are starting to see the light and look into the online influencer market. And they will be right because this sector is currently hot! They realised that apart from the famous celebrities they have been in partnership with, they could also engage children when it comes to the release of the hottest toys, children's clothes and stuff. This could encourage other children to give 'kidfluencing' a try when they see videos and adverts of peers doing it.

Now take Ryan's World for example. 'Ryan's World is a YouTube channel and brand that features a young boy named Ryan and his family creating kid-friendly content like toy unboxing, gaming, and science experiments', says Narciso.[94] Ryan's World achieved success by offering relatable and enjoyable content. It tapped into the Gen Alpha audience's fascination with children their own age playing with toys and participating in exciting activities, effectively meeting this demand. Additionally, the brand harnessed the influence of well-known Gen Alpha brands, YouTubers, and social media celebrities through strategic partnerships.

Other social media accounts like Call Me Sparkle and Zooey in the City are some of the most popular accounts among social media users. Basically, these accounts are about the advertisement of different kinds and styles of youth fashion. Those who are interested in outdoor adventure will probably be obsessed with Hawkeye Huey's account. These accounts, to some people, are a way for youngsters to show what their various interests are while giving them the opportunity to earn some money. It's also known that some parents, in fact, create the accounts for their children. Apparently, some people still oppose this method, as they believe that the parents are indirectly using their children as a source of income. Nevertheless, many young people still enjoy their work as a kid influencer.

Gen ZAlphas have been raised in a world filled with technology, a very different experience compared to their parents and older generations. They're known for being social, global, and mobile because they have done everything through various digital channels – since they were born. The internet has a big impact on them, and they're even influencing what their parents buy. This means that businesses need to think about both making things and advertising them if they want a supply chain that's honest and ethical. They are more diverse than any other generation, so businesses that include everyone are important to them. Not paying attention to this micro-generation would be a mistake, as they're the future. Companies should be ready with the right tools and ways to catch their interest and do well in the next ten years. They should invest in ways to engage customers, like using automation for marketing and finding out quickly how their messages are landing? Using data to make their communication better will help them understand what customers like and do, and even predict what they'll want in the future.[27]

> 'Where Gen Z still demands that the digital experience approaches the real experience, Gen ZAlpha will be the generation that demands that the real experience offers at least as much as it does in the digital world.'

Collecting Data From Gen ZAlpha

In April 2010, Steve Jobs introduced the very first iPad, marking a significant milestone. Apple's hardware innovations played a pivotal role in driving children's increasing online presence in recent years. Many young parents, myself included, embraced the iPad as an ideal educational tool for their kids. Consequently, children's online activity has surged dramatically.

To put this into perspective, every second, two children venture online for the first time. That equates to a staggering 7,200 new young internet users every hour, forming a daily cohort of approximately 170,000 children. Notably, children now constitute around 40% of all new internet users. They serve as the driving force behind the growth of numerous consumer apps and services.

However, the internet, as we currently know it, presents a significant challenge for children. Content discovery on the web relies heavily on algorithms. When kids search online, they encounter content suggestions, often including material unsuitable for their age.

The central predicament is that the internet was not initially designed with children in mind, as the assumption was that this young audience would not be exposed to such content. Consequently, kids are inadvertently exposed to a plethora of inappropriate material.

Furthermore, our digital footprint begins as soon as we step into the online realm. Every time we visit a website, launch an app, or engage with platforms like YouTube, Facebook, or TikTok, we are subject to extensive tracking technology. Eventually, advertising technology transforms our preferences and behaviours into personalised ads and offers.

Over the course of our digital lives, a substantial amount of our personal data floats across the internet. In November 2018, a significant report titled 'Who Knows What About Me' shed light on how major tech companies collect data from children. The report, published by Anne Longfield, England's Children's Commissioner tasked with safeguarding children's rights, scrutinises the potential hazards associated with the data amassed by tech giants.

KidTech: The Rise of a New Tech Industry

While working on this book, I came across an emerging movement known as Kidtech, spearheaded by visionary pioneers. One of these trailblazers is Dylan Collins, the CEO and Co-founder of Super Awesome, a leading Kidtech company. Super Awesome's technology serves as a safeguard, allowing content providers and brands to interact with children online while ensuring their complete safety and anonymity. This innovation enables brands to connect with their audience and empowers content providers to disseminate their material securely.

Kidtech is rapidly gaining prominence as a critical technology for facilitating online engagement with Generation ZAlpha. In addition to Super Awesome, various networks and tools, such as Kidscorp, Yoki, Playwire, Freewheel, Precise TV within the YouTube ecosystem, as well as identity management solutions like Privo, Twohat, and Crisp's content moderation, are all contributing to creating a more comfortable and secure online environment for children.

This movement is characterised by two fundamental principles: privacy by design, ensuring that children have online privacy – a legal requirement globally, and the commitment to providing a safe and high-quality online experience for children. It embodies the vision of Internet 3.0 – a safer, improved internet tailored for the wellbeing of children.

As Dylan Collins aptly puts it, 'If we make the internet better and safer for children, we make it better for everybody.'

The Perception of Gaming through Decades

Older generations have always distrusted progress since ancient times. In The Republic, Plato claimed that plays and poems had a negative impact on young people. Similarly, a thousand years ago, when writing became technically easier and more accessible, 'wise elders' warned that the ability to write would adversely affect the intellect of future generations, as they would no longer need to remember information and train their memory. With the development of printing, fears spread among the adult population that printed novels were corrupting young people, especially girls. The radio would turn us deaf, and when televisions appeared in every home, the programmes were often accused of causing irreparable physical, psychological and social damage to future generations.

Today, video games often seem to be the target as they are associated with a variety of horrors. Games cause depression, physical aggression, brain degradation and attention disorders, and gamers all suffer from sleep deprivation and obesity.

Family and Video Games

Millennials had their era with Facebook, and Generation Z embraced TikTok. Similarly, Generation Alpha is identified as the Minecraft or Roblox generation. Scientists at the University of Montreal performed several pieces of research and concluded that video games cannot be considered generally harmful or generally useful – the way they act on the brain, many effects depend on the game itself and the characteristics of a particular person.

Even though there's proof that technology can have bad effects on children, Gen ZAlpha's parents trust and welcome technology more than any previous generation of parents. Millennials were the first kids to grow up with digital technology, spending time in AIM chat rooms with people they didn't know and posting their photos on Myspace. While parents try to protect their kids from parts of tech that are too grown-up, they also like the good things about it. Actually, when we asked Millennial parents which brands they trust most for their kids, four out of the top five were technology brands: YouTube (53%), Netflix (48%), Amazon (42%), and Google (39%). They often have family movie nights where they watch videos and movies on YouTube and Netflix. Millennials used to ask their parents for gadgets when they were young, but they didn't often get them. This made them spend more on gadgets for their own kids, and they enjoy games and videos just as much.

We've noticed that more teenagers are playing simulation games (like real-life and building games) lately. These kinds of games have become the fourth most popular type of game among 12- to 15-year-olds, moving ahead of fighting and sports since 2021. Kids really like what these games offer: the chance to think and learn, and work together with others.

This is especially true for younger kids: more 8- to 11-year-olds want to use building tools than 12- to 15-year-olds (49% vs. 37%), and the same goes for Minecraft (65% vs. 50%). This might be because younger kids are naturally more into creative things like arts and crafts, space, and playing dress-up.

> '57% of 8- to 11-year-olds in the US prefer to play games for social interactions.'
>
> (GWI, 2022)[103]

Fortnite, Minecraft, Roblox and Zepeto are incredibly popular amongst kids and teenagers. While Minecraft, Roblox and Zepeto let you design and create in a fictional world, Fortnite is a survival game. Roblox and Zepeto are also metaverse platforms. These games or platforms often have supportive online communities that are always available for help.

1. Fortnite

Fortnite stands as a survival game in which a hundred players engage in player versus player combat, aiming to be the last one remaining. This high-paced, action-packed game resembles The Hunger Games, demanding strategic thought for survival. About 125 million players are estimated to be involved in Fortnite. Although it is rated for ages 12 and above, age verification isn't required when creating an account, and it's widely known that many Alpha children are avid Fortnite players.

Upon parachuting onto a small island, players are armed only with an axe and must scavenge for additional weapons, all while evading a deadly electrical storm. As players are eliminated, the playable area becomes smaller, forcing remaining players closer together. Frequent updates flash on the screen, describing how one player eliminated another – phrases like 'X killed Y with a grenade' – adding to the suspense.

Fortnite Battle Royale is a fiercely competitive game of survival. Victory requires defeating the other 99 online players in the match. Players must also evade being caught in the storm's path to stay in the game; countdowns alert them to the approaching storm. The game's vibrant animations and graphics are particularly appealing to younger users. There's also an element of fun, with options to purchase Christmas and dinosaur costumes. Avatars can even perform dance moves using the 'Emote' feature. These dances can be activated during the game, adding a touch of amusement. Many of these dances are inspired by popular culture, allowing players to enjoy them both in-game and outside, like in the schoolyard.

At the same time, Fortnite appears to be losing its popularity somehow. Forbes writer Paul Tassi noticed mid-2019 that the Google search trends for Fortnite had declined steadily in the preceding few months.

2. Minecraft

Best for ages eight and up, this is an open-ended environment focused on exploration and creation that lets players create items and buildings from scratch, using only materials they harvest from the world around them.

Research on children who played Minecraft showed positive results, such as the development of abstract thinking, self-reflection, communication skills, increased resistance, empathy and feelings of self-reflection.

12-year-old Minecraft is one of the most played games in the world, attracting more than 90 million players a month. Children can play it with friends, multiplatform, across consoles and on iOS and Android. Often called 'virtual LEGO', the idea is to mine and construct three-dimensional blocks in various worlds and different terrains, learning skills along the way such as reasoning, problem-solving, and collaboration.

Additionally, kids are motivated to gather and pile up blocks in order to generate food, tools, and animals. This process assists them in constructing a feeling of determination and self-identity. YouTube vloggers who engage in Minecraft serve as authentic sources of encouragement for players by providing them with helpful advice and techniques. Moreover, users have the ability to construct and investigate within the actual world, crafting and exchanging their creations with their friends.

> 'Every lake is a place you can fish in, every park is a place where you can chop down trees. We've actually taken maps of the entire world and converted them to Minecraft.'
>
> Torfi Olafsson,
> Game director

3. Roblox

Roblox is a multi-user online platform that allows children, of ages ten and up, to create their own games. Sometimes compared to Minecraft, Roblox is a website and an application that hosts virtual world games in a social network, built from Lego-like virtual blocks.

With games like Roblox, children can create any world they can imagine and communicate with other players around the world. Children spend hundreds of hours playing games like Roblox, and they are emotionally connected to their accounts to a level that many adults do not even know about. Taking into account the possibilities and creativity which Roblox provides to children, the company-manufacturer takes an active position to protect its players from unwanted content, online hackers, cybertheft and other internet dangers. Roblox provides resources such as in-game moderation, content control and guidance for parents. A study by Raz-Fridman[32] provides an analysis of Roblox's recent earnings report and highlights several key findings.

- Roblox's user base continues to grow at a rapid pace. The platform had 267 million monthly active users in Q4 2022, up 39% from the same period the previous year. This growth was driven by both new user acquisition and increased engagement from existing users.
- Roblox's revenue is also increasing at a significant rate. The platform generated $1.4 billion in revenue in Q4 2022, up 46% from the same period the previous year. This growth was driven by an increase in bookings, which is the total amount of money spent by users on the platform. Bookings grew 58% year-over-year to $1.9 billion.
- Roblox is expanding beyond its core gaming business. The company is investing in new areas such as virtual concerts, digital merchandise, and educational content. This diversification is aimed at attracting new users and increasing engagement among existing users.
- Roblox is seeing strong growth in its international markets. The platform's user base outside of North America and Europe grew 54% year-on-year, driven by growth in markets such as Asia and Latin America.
- Roblox is investing heavily in infrastructure to support its growth. The company is building out its cloud infrastructure and investing in data analytics to improve the user experience and drive engagement.

Roblox's earnings report is a positive sign for the platform's future growth. The company's user base and revenue are both increasing at a significant rate, and the company is investing in new areas to diversify its business and attract new users – which is possible through partnerships, like Fenty Beauty below for example.

Rihanna has extended the reach of Fenty Beauty into the metaverse by collaborating with Roblox, enabling players to explore and interact with the brand's virtual products. This marks just one of the various initiatives undertaken by beauty brands to captivate younger audiences through gamified encounters on digital platforms.[104]

However, recent research shows that Roblox is not exactly an all-age friendly game, which might be alarming for parents of Alphas.

'I just spent six hours playing the games meant for 5-year-olds and it was freaking awful,' writes Carolyn Velociraptor, a mother and an influencer. 'Something is very wrong with Roblox Corp.' She found out that the game allows children to visit some weird environments inside the game. Velociraptor wrote in a twitter thread, which has gone viral, that the game allows avatars to get partially naked while other avatars are watching, which is disturbing to watch for a teenager or a 10- year-old. She came across some other bizarre events inside the game which she called out, and asked the designers of the game and other parents to take note of these disturbing features.[33]

4. Zepeto

Zepeto is a South-Korean mobile app that allows users to create personalised 3D avatars of themselves and to interact in different virtual worlds. These avatars can be customised in various ways, including hairstyles, outfits, and accessories, to resemble the user's appearance and style. Zepeto also offers a virtual social platform where users can interact with their friends' avatars and engage in virtual activities such as taking pictures, playing mini-games, and exploring virtual spaces. The social aspect of Zepeto is a key feature that encourages engagement and connectivity among users.

Zepeto has its own in-app currency called 'Zems'. Users can earn Zems by participating in activities, completing missions, or purchasing them through microtransactions. Zems can be used to buy virtual items, accessories, and clothing to further customise avatars.

Zepeto frequently hosts events and collaborations with various brands, influencers, and celebrities. These events can include special avatar items, themed virtual spaces, and other interactive experiences. It helps keep the platform fresh and engaging for users.

Zepeto has a global user base, and it gained popularity, especially among younger audiences who enjoy creating and customising avatars for social interactions.

YouTube

For many, YouTube has become a substitute for television, while it also remains the cheapest option to keep the child entertained. YouTube appeared in 2005 in San Bruno and was created by former employees of PayPal. In 2006, Google bought YouTube for 1.65 billion dollars, thus becoming its owner. Many celebrities and large companies have official channels on YouTube, and videos from YouTube are often shown in official television reports. Today, the site is the most popular video hosting in the world, replenished with hundreds of new videos every minute. Millions of viewers visit it daily.

In 2019, Google and YouTube settled a lawsuit by agreeing to pay a historic $170 million. The lawsuit alleged that the companies were violating the Children's Online Privacy Protection Act (COPPA) by collecting personal information from children without parental consent. The settlement required YouTube to develop a system to identify content directly aimed at children, ensuring compliance with COPPA. In response, YouTube made changes to platform features for kid-targeted videos, including the removal of personalised ads and disabling video comments. While children's advocacy groups considered these changes a small yet positive step, many YouTube creators feared revenue loss, sparking a

'COPPAcalypse' panic in the YouTuber community. This fear was confirmed as channel owners reported significant revenue drops of 60 to 75 percent.

Pocket Watch, on the other hand, manages a diverse network of industry relationships, generating revenue through various streams beyond YouTube video ads. Through Pocket Watch's support, eight-year-old Ryan has expanded his brand with clothing, toy lines, a Nickelodeon show, a smartphone app, a video game, and five related YouTube channels. Ryan's growth exemplifies Pocket Watch's vision to transform top-performing family YouTube channels into multi-category global franchises.

Aligned with a broader trend, Pocket Watch extends young influencers' reach beyond digital media to material culture and consumption, turning them into global consumers of commercial products within a neoliberal framework.

YouTube serves various purposes for users, from entertainment to learning and publishing videos. This generation heavily engages with YouTube, using it for learning, entertainment, relaxation, and comfort. Recent USA research indicates that Alphas prefer watching YouTube over television programmes. A significant percentage of parents, 57% with children aged 2 or younger and 81% with kids aged 3 or 4, reported that their children watch videos on YouTube.[35]

YouTube Kidfluencers

YouTube Kids, a specialised app created by Google for young viewers, has been widely embraced by kids who enjoy watching videos on YouTube. The app provides a wide selection of age-appropriate content, allowing kids to navigate through videos using swipe gestures or category menus. It's designed to offer curated, ad-supported TV shows, music, educational content, and user-generated videos. Individual user profiles can be created for each child, tailoring the content to their respective ages.

The app includes a 'Learning' section with educational clips from reputable sources like Khan Academy, PBS Kids, and TED-Ed. The 'Explore' section offers a diverse range of user-generated content, toy-related videos, and a variety of kid-friendly material, including brand-sponsored channels like McDonald's. However, studies by Common Sense Media in 2020 have revealed that the majority of videos watched by young children are primarily for entertainment rather than education. Additionally, inappropriate content sometimes appears in the videos, including violence targeted at older audiences.

88% of parents whose children watch content on YouTube
say it helps them learn new things. (Pew Research Center, 2020)[102]

> '88% of parents whose children watch content on
> YouTube say it helps them learn new things.'
>
> (Pew Research Center, 2020)[102]

Google has taken measures to improve content curation since the app's launch in 2015. Human monitors are engaged to personally review flagged videos, and 'verified' videos are offered as reliable options. Parents are given the option to block and report inappropriate content and ads. However, the app occasionally displays ads that might obstruct educational content or resemble recommended videos. Parents can choose between allowing their kids to search freely or relying on age-based content settings, which provide generally suitable videos for specific age groups.

Despite these efforts, the app may still have shortcomings. It's advised to watch videos together with younger children or wait until they're slightly more mature due to potential commercialism, inappropriate content, and disturbing videos that may slip through. The issue of disturbing videos is particularly concerning. Some videos that appear kid-friendly at first can take disturbing turns. These videos, known as 'YouTube Poop', manipulate tags to deceive the algorithm. Although Google has taken steps to address this issue, some inappropriate content still surfaces. However, the addition of human monitors and improved content review processes should aid in mitigating these concerns.

About Influencing

Children on YouTube and Instagram aim to be gamers, video bloggers, DIYers and fashionistas, or they own family channels, which are often a cross between

GENERATION ZAlpha

reality shows, pranks, and random scenes. Their accounts can generate serious revenue without dealing with brands. As unobtrusive as they may look at first sight, these channels have all the characteristics of influence marketing: the promotion of brands and their products with the help of stars, but addressing the audience directly without the usual advertising format.

The digital social network has become fertile ground for retailers looking for ways to push their goods. A large number of social influencers , with the help of companies, promote parent-friendly products, kitchen and bathroom appliances or all sorts of toys.

Many children want to become YouTube tastemakers, and they all start by creating their own content. If their videos become viral, and they decide to expand, parents often help to edit and promote the video through other social platforms. Brands want to work with children for the same reasons they want to work with adults in social networks: the number of subscribers and the ability to publish messages faster than via traditional advertising agencies. Parents of kidfluencers claim that brands can pay from $10,000 to $15,000 for an advertising post on Instagram, while a YouTube video can yield $45,000. Exposure from thirty to ninety seconds in a longer video can cost advertisers anything from $15,000 to $25,000.

'I am not sure if you can make a living off of Instagram. Some might be doing it, but I think you are more likely to make a living off YouTube. But, I know that is a lot of work because you have to post new content daily to stay relevant and that could be stressful. I post on Instagram once or twice a week, and that alone is a lot of work, while I have to be a wife, mom, housewife, cook, etc. ☺ hahaha.'

Sandra,
mother of Ryan
Instagram kidfluencer
128k followers
USA

The growth of this type of advertising has prompted questions concerning fair compensation, supervision, and work permits, especially since the recommendations on child labour vary from country to country.

> 'I see a lot of competition on Instagram among other moms rather than kids. I do not like to surround myself around that because you should be your own competition only, and be better than you were yesterday and not anybody else ...'
>
> Sandra,
> mother of Ryan
> Instagram kidfluencer
> 128k followers
> USA

But at the same time, not all our participants agree that there is any competition among the influencers.

> '...I don't think there is a lot of competition. This is amazing, but I feel that we mothers understand and support each other. It really feels like we know each other in real life too.'
>
> Cissi Fioriniello,
> mother of Amelia (3) and Bianca (1)
> Instagram mummy-blogger (58k)
> Sweden

An Instagram spokeswoman, Sravanthi Dev, said that even though the online platform does not allow users under thirteen to create profiles, their parents or official representatives can create profiles for them, 'as long as it is clear in the biographical information that the account is run by the parent or representative'. As for children, it can be challenging for them to understand how much excitement they create. 'When you see the analytics of a kidfluencer channel, the dominant audience consists of 25- to 34-year-old women. That's obviously not the case. Rather, the child is watching it on their parents' device,' says Mr Chavez-Munoz, a founder of Viral Talent.

The success of all these rising stars on social media is the result of their parents' business initiative. Instead of impromptu photoshoots, parents dress up their babies or toddlers and arrange professional photo sessions.

> 'I was posting photos of Ryan on my personal Instagram when he was only a year old. It was reposted on FashionKids Instagram, and it went viral from there.'
>
> Sandra,
> mother of Ryan
> Instagram kidfluencer
> 128k followers
> USA

> '...this looks easy, but it's a lot of work. I always have a pictured idea in my head before I choose clothes or have a collab with brands. Then I need to fix everything, bring my idea to life, but sometimes doesn't work how I thought it would.'
>
> Cissi Fioriniello,
> mother of Amelia (3) and Bianca (1)
> Instagram mummy-blogger (58k)
> Sweden

Defining boundaries between game and work may be hard. There are no guidelines that regulate earnings for children on the internet. All responsibility is delegated to the parents, who are managing their kidfluencers.

The Influence an Influencer Can Have

The power of social media can be illustrated in one single story. In February 2018, Kylie Jenner posted a Twitter post asking if anyone else was using Snapchat or not. Users reacted with lightning speed: thousands of likes and hundreds of repostings, as is usually the case, spread across the microblogging site in mere seconds. This one random (or non-random) post plunged Snapchat's market value by 6.1 percent, which in dollars amounted to $1.3 billion. Eighteen words published on a social network can ruin a large company, if only they are said by a person who is backed by hundreds of millions of subscribers.

Many of the interviewed parents said that their children either do not know about Instagram or mostly think of it as being funny footage with their mother. The older members of the Alpha generation have a more unobstructed view.

'When people say to you that you are a role model
to them and that they love our daughter,
my heart gets full of love, and we are even more
motivated to continue our work. For me, this is just
the proof that we are doing our job right :)'

Vjosa Muriqi,
mother of Artina Dea (1)
Instagram mummy-blogger (159k)
Stuttgart, Germany

'I feel like I just post pictures but hard to believe
that people really buy similar or identical clothes. But
sometimes, they send me pictures or tag me, so I can
see it. This is amazing.'

Cissi Fioriniello,
mother of Amelia (3) and Bianca (1)
Instagram mummy-blogger (58k)
Sweden

> 'I do understand the influence that my media pages have on children and their parents. I actually love that I get to express my thoughts and opinions through fashion.'
>
> Haileigh Vasquez
> 10-year-old
> Instagram kidfluencer (128k)
> New York, USA

How Different Types of Influencers Build Relationships with Children

To some, the reason why children watch other people play video games is a mystery, as it might not be their area of interest. But to those who are whole-heartedly interested in watching, the influencers are doing a pretty good job by keeping them entertained, and these influencers definitely mean a lot to these young viewers. Influencers not only win the hearts and minds of their fans and gain a reputation for themselves, they also influence the choices their fans make. These influencers tend to guide their watchers, who are usually younger than thirteen, on what to buy.

Influencers, in general, have their own different personalities and they each express theirs in their topics of interests. Some, or rather, most of these interests tend to be stereotypical in nature, and include hobbies like crafting. When it comes to gamers, they tend to keep the atmosphere goofy.

Insight Kids conducted research on a population of 1,200 American children and parents to understand these types of personalities. Their research has shown that not all influencers are the same, and their characters can be divided into four main personalities, which are: The Superfan, The Buddy, The Firecracker, and The Icon.

1. The Superfan

Superfans are really good at connecting with kids online. They use facts and show that they know what they're talking about, which makes kids trust them.

They're like experts, and even if they don't like something, they're still honest about it. This honesty is really important for kids. Superfans show up in lots of different areas and they're important for new influencers. This helps them build a good reputation and show what they're good at. For instance, influencers who are into music can give kids something that inspires them.

Video: Pentatonix never misses a note.
https://www.youtube.com/watch?v=xicTgODBJIE

2. The Buddy

This type of personality is friendly and easy to connect with. They share their own experiences and findings to help young viewers improve their skills. Kids often see them as regular people who are always kind. They suggest other videos to watch, what products to buy, and how to get better at things. They take their time so even younger kids can follow along.

This personality works well for influencers who make food, drinks, snacks, crafts, and DIY projects. Kids want these online influencers to show that they really understand what they're doing because they know making these things can be challenging.

Video: Karina Garcia isn't afraid to mess up and makes
the best of her mistakes.
https://www.youtube.com/watch?v=p-SAT8FfkQI

3. The Firecracker

This personality trait makes kids feel like they're part of the exciting things happening in the video. The influencers are funny and full of energy, which makes kids even more excited to watch. They also try to talk to their fans and answer their questions, making kids feel like they're connected to the influencer. These influencers talk directly to the camera, do Q&A sessions, reply to messages, and even like their fans' posts.

Many influencers with this trait give their fans special names, like 'victors' or 'gamers'. This makes kids feel like they're part of a special group. Influencers with this personality do well because they bring a lot of excitement and energy to their fans, especially in gaming videos.

Video: Dan TDM, a videogame influencer, often responds directly to fans and has a whimsical approach.
https://www.youtube.com/watch?v=Q2D9OEWgWaU

4. The Icon

This personality trait is all about style and being perfect. These influencers are really good at showing their unique qualities and creating their own brand. They use catchy phrases or have creative ways of looking and sounding. They spend a lot of time on FaceTime, often with their regular friends or other people. Many of them ask for likes and have followers who help them promote their own brands.

Unlike the Buddy personality trait, who is very kind, the icon could be quite different and might choose to be unlikable or rude, but in a way that's entertaining. Kids might not be super excited about this personality trait, but they could still be influenced by the way the product is presented, how it all fits together, and the special things that make the influencer stand out.

This personality trait is often a good fit for fashion lovers or people who are really into technology. Social media storytellers can also be great icons, although sometimes they also show the firecracker personality trait.

HypeAuditor Perspectives on Influencers

That's it for influencers, but how can brands track their activities? HypeAuditor it is. The HypeAuditor service implements comprehensive information about Instagram influencers using artificial intelligence to provide an Audience Quality Score (AQS) – an indicator that combines several metrics. The developers got the idea to create an influencer marketplace where brands can meet the influencer. Back in the summer of 2019, they launched the same analytical tool for YouTube.

According to Anna Komok (marketing and PR manager), the kidfluential market is growing at a very fast rate in Asia. Compared to Instagram engagement worldwide, participation in the East is twice as big. Plus, the audience is much more active, despite China's 'Golden Shield Project' limiting internet access, with enormous consequences for their presence to the social media market. People there learned to use VPN to get access to social media platforms, and the Instagram audience is still on the rise.

Over the past years, there is definitely an increase in numbers when we are talking about the kidfluencer market. 'It was interesting to find out that content for children is not so polished when we compare it to other influencers. They do not have these glamorous filters and photographs. They just post stuff like what they eat and what they see, and the reaction to this content is not meaningful or particularly expressive,' says Anna Komok.

'Children usually leave a one-word comment like 'cool', or just send emoji. They are not used to writing long comments or asking questions on social media. Most of the time, they have a short, quick reaction. Therefore, it is tough to analyse them because their responses are akin to the words of answering bots! It's like they're copying them.'

The average engagement rate among kidfluencers is significantly higher when they have between 1000 and 5000 followers. In some regions, such as the US,

Canada, and France, the engagement tripled in comparison with those who have more than 20,000 followers. In countries like Russia, Germany and Iran, the engagement is in four times higher within the group with under 5000 followers.

As for the 'likes', the statistics show us the opposite result. A significant leap in the proportional number of likes among kid influencers is most noticeable within the group who have more than 20,000 followers. For instance, the average influencer post in Turkey gets 369 likes, while those who are in the range from 20,000 to 100,000 followers get around 1140 likes per post. In Malaysia, this ranges between 498 and 1175 likes per post.

As for payment, different patterns can be discerned per region. According to the HypeAuditor, most of the time, it depends on the audience size. For instance, those with up to 20,000 subscribers on Instagram and up to 100,000 on YouTube can still agree to barter for products, but not always. In the CIS they are more willing to go on barter, while in the UK and the US, even with 5K subscribers on Instagram, most likely, they will ask for money. Prominent bloggers, no matter whether children or adults, charge money or money + products in the case of review. In this context, it is important to note 90% of them have agents who deal with these issues.

Academic Perspectives on Influencers

Over the next ten years, the influencer market will reach its glory days, but at the same time, there is a high probability that there is going to be a downturn, claims Liselot Hudders, assistant professor at Ghent University. And there are several reasons for it. First, let us have a look at the core mechanisms of influencer marketing from a theoretical point of view.

Liselot Hudders claims that 'influencers are perceived as highly credible sources of information, and people tend to follow their advice. People consider these influencers as their friends, and they believe that they give a genuine recommendation in their social media posts. Accordingly, they believe that the recommendation is more honest compared to a brand post, and this reliability causes higher effectiveness. Moreover, by interacting with the influencer, followers enter into so-called parasocial interaction with the influencer.' These interactions, which elicit feelings of connectedness, combined with a sneak peek into the private life of the influencer, make influencers highly persuasive sources. And finally, most people do not consider Instagram celebrities as a source of advertising and do not feel like they are being manipulated, because sponsored posts are often not labelled correctly and perfectly fit in the story.

Professor Hudders states that many do not use a proper sponsorship disclosure (e.g. #advertising) or hide it among the other hashtags. They often disguise the commercial intent of the post because they are afraid that they will lose their credibility. However, people become more aware of sponsored content as it becomes omnipresent on Instagram, especially when you see 10 different stories of one influencer endorsing different brands in one day. *'So people become knowledgeable about the tactic. And I think it will become less effective,'* she says.

These days, it is quite common for influencers to have many unpaid collaborations. For instance, brands could invite them to a party or to visit foreign countries and take a photoshoot. Companies often offer influencers a free flight, a hotel and sometimes an outfit, but without any additional financial compensation for their work. Even the big influencers are doing a lot of free collaborations because they strive to build an attractive profile and get more followers, in the hope that one day, other brands will offer them lucrative contracts.

> 'Personally, I do believe that brands should act more responsibly when initiating such collaborations. The responsible involvement of influencers in the marketing strategy is an issue that should be dealt with on a global level, especially when child influencers are involved. For example, when children are hired as actors, they get a contract and adequate support, so for an influencer, this should be the same.'
>
> she concludes.

> 'For me, as well as for my colleagues, it sounds quite striking, and it worries me because it sounds like free labour – such companies use Instagram stars as models, but do not pay for the modelling.'
>
> says Liselot Hudders.

In the case of kidfluencers, the risks of unpaid labour are even higher because parents want to get free gear for their children, not always realising that by the time they come of age, their child will have a life that has been entirely documented and out in the open for millions of people to see.

According to Hudders, there is a significant difference between kidfluencers and the children of celebrities. In the celebrity atmosphere, people have a public appearance, and the press may take some pictures, but their private life can be hidden from the general public. Influencers, in contrast, show many aspects of their private lives where children do everyday things like watching television, going to school, or spending time with their friends and family and other special moments.

As for the parents of influencers, Hudders suggests they need to be protected from negativity as well as from praise. This is a common issue for teens at school, because when you are a celebrity and receive presents from famous brands, then other children become jealous, and that can lead to cyberbullying.

There are two significant issues related to this market. First, sponsored content is often not recognised as advertising. This is because the sponsored content is not correctly disclosed, and the exact commercial relationship with the brand and influencer is not clearly defined. The second is that the influencers have full self-responsibility for their content, or at least, these are the rules in Belgium. Therefore, they can, for instance, get sued for unlawful discriminatory material.

Liselot Hudders also provides a brilliant example of how influencers and kidfluencers can be involved in social issues. Liselot and her colleagues noticed that many of the food bloggers do not offer healthy meals. This aroused their curiosity – what if they could use influencers as social marketing agents to help children change their behaviour for the better?

At this time, you can already see some social marketing collaborations with celebrities like the 'meatless days' campaign in Belgium (#dagenzondervlees). The goal is to boost awareness, inspiration and behavioural change around sustainable food and reducing meat consumption. This is not the only example of non-profit organisations that try to recruit influences as their ambassadors.

Research also shows that kids who use social media more often than their peers are less sensitive towards rewards and punishments and they are more anxious about social situations. By contrast, children who have lesser social media usage are more sensitive about punishments and rewards and care highly about being liked by their peers.[37]

Let's Meet Some Kidpreneurs

Riley Kinnane-Petersen, age 13

'When I grow up, I want to continue my business. But if not, then I might become a chemist. Or a vet.'

Riley Kinnane-Petersen is a 13-year-old kidfluencer who started the business with the help of her two dads. They collected unwanted jewellery from their friends and family. Riley then dismantled that jewellery to make new designs and sold them off at front yard lemonade stands.

Seven years later, she's now running a business named Gunner & Lux, that has Nordstorm and J.Crew among its high profile customers. She promotes girl power through her business by selling t-shirts with slogans like 'All of my heroes are women' and 'My dad is a feminist'.

Oliver 'Ollie' Fequiere, age 9

'I watched the Black Spider-Man in Into the Spider-Verse – I have seen it many times. He is brown, and he lives in New York. And I have the Spider-Man costume too. We have a lot of things in common.'

Oliver is a 9-year-old boy who relies on his parents to run his business named Fizzie and Fables. It is a bath and storytime business. He also makes the bath fizzies and does the packaging as well. Ollie manages everything from idea to product testing. His parents help him in all of this. He doesn't know what he wants to become when he grows up but is definitely working on building an exceptional resume.

Jahkil Jackson, age 15

Jakhil is a 15-year-old motivational speaker and a best-selling author. He is motivated to inspire children all across the country to help the needy and make a difference in their communities. During Covid-19, Jakhil encouraged more than 200 youngsters from 70 countries to create and distribute blessing bags to those in need. His mission is to collaborate with more like-minded young people, motivate them to discover their passions, and continue to work to make this world a better place. To fulfil his goals, Jakhil raises funds from the public to procure supplies and cover shipping costs. He gained recognition as a Youth Ambassador for Heartland Alliance during the summer of 2016 for his initiative 'Project I am.' Joining the WE International Youth Council in 2017, he committed himself to global betterment. Jahkil also had the honour of speaking at WE Day, an event that celebrates young changemakers positively impacting both local and global communities.

In 2018, Jahkil became the youngest member of the Independent Youth group, which empowers young individuals to pave the way as future business leaders and innovative entrepreneurs. His extraordinary accomplishments include his appointment as Vice Chairman of the 2019 KidBox Youth Board of Directors and Chairman of the Dreams for Kids Youth Executive Board. BET recognised his achievements by naming him one of their '15 under 15' honourees. Notably, President Barack Obama and the Obama Foundation identified Jahkil as one of the influential figures in 2017.

Jahkil has actively participated in impactful campaigns, including Disney's Be Inspired Black History Campaign, LeBron James's #AlwaysBelieve 2018 campaign, and Nike's Until We All Win & You Can't Stop Our Voice campaigns. His contributions have earned him the distinction of being recognised as a Marvel Super Hero and CNN Heroes: Young Wonder. His philanthropic efforts caught the attention of major brands such as Crate & Barrel, Invisalign, and The Gap, who chose him as a representative for their Gen Z campaigns.

When asked about how he got the courage to start all of this Jakhil says: 'I wasn't really scared. I actually had a lot of support, and I was all pumped to do it. I was like this super happy, energetic kid. Mom will probably disagree.'

Piper Williams, age 11

At the age of 4, Piper didn't like to wear panties designed for girls, so she had an idea of developing a clothing line that produces boxer shorts for girls. She is now 11 years old and her business is already thriving. Her whole family supported her idea because of which 'My Pipers' is a recognised brand.

> 'A lot of kids think it's really cool, and we have teachers who have our hoodies. And a lot of our friends wear our boxer shorts.'
>
> Piper says on the popularity of her clothing line.

Lily Harper, age 9

Lily is one of the youngest entrepreneurs. She started her business in 2021 when she was only 7 years old. Her mom decided to pull her out of school because she was being bullied, but traditional home-schooling also turned out difficult. At that point they had an idea of starting a business named as 'Lily Lou's Aromas'.

Lily loves wax melts and candles. After she dropped school and found out that traditional home-schooling did not work for her, her grandmother suggested the idea of learning through play. That's when she started her business with the help of her mom. They made candles for themselves at the start, somebody saw those and asked if Lily could produce on order. This sparked the idea of 'Lily Lou's Aromas'.

When she was asked about the future of her business, she said:

> 'My next big goal for my business is to own a warehouse and be in big stores!'

Sophia Fairweather, age 14

Sophia is a passionate champion of youth entrepreneurship. Despite being in sixth grade, she has gained recognition as a speaker at international events. Supported by her father, she actively advocates for economic development organisations to establish additional grants and opportunities specifically tailored for young entrepreneurs.

Sophia's journey as an entrepreneur began when she was just 5 years old. She approached her father with an innovative idea: a hook-and-loop product designed to hold phones securely in place. This initial creation, FunCro, marked the beginning of a series of inventions for this young enthusiast with a keen interest in STEM. When she is not immersed in her business endeavours, Sophia enjoys activities such as swimming, drawing, and indulging in episodes of Stargate.

The Gill Brothers

Austin and his brothers started a business under the guidance of their mum – Celena – who is also a small business owner and a former teacher.

Austin, Collin and Ryan are not your typical 8-year-olds. Instead of choosing usual childhood activities, they chose to start their own candle business called 'Frères Branchiaux'. When they approached their parents for money to buy some toys, their parents asked them to either get a job or start a business; they chose the latter.

Celena, alongside their home-schooling, was also teaching them business concepts like supply chain, customer service and marketing practically through their own business. Austin and his brothers also donate 10 percent of their profits to a local shelter for homeless people.

The Gill brothers' entrepreneurial spirit comes from a family history of small business ownership. Celena's grandfather was one of the first black mechanic shop owners in Virginia, and her extended family members always had side gigs. Starting the candle business was a way for the Gill brothers to create their own opportunities.

Frères Branchiaux began with handmade candles and later expanded to an online presence. The brothers are actively involved in the day-to-day operations, from making the candles to managing sales at markets. Their mother emphasises that the boys' wellbeing and priorities come first, and the business doesn't run seven days a week. Collin will eventually take over the business when he turns 18, but for now, Celena is still the legal guardian and supports of their entrepreneurial journey.

As the business grows, the family is considering hiring more staff and moving operations out of their home. The Gill brothers are enjoying the financial benefits of their business, with Austin even purchasing an electric scooter. While their future aspirations vary, with interests in architecture, professional football, and basketball, owning a candle business is already a part of their identity.

Perlyn Brothers, age 7 and 10

The Perlyn brothers, Ethan (10 years old) and Merritt (7 years old), are not only passionate about surfing and sports but are also young entrepreneurs. They started their surf-inspired company called Crepic, which is now a year old. Their hats and accessories are sold in several stores, and the brothers consider themselves the bosses of the business.

They love to paddleboard, surf and play soccer, basketball, and video games like Fortnite. They share their pride in running Crepic for a year and their enthusiasm for donating a portion of their proceeds to bullying prevention.

Their parents supported their business idea and helped them in learning about Shopify. After that they built their own website from scratch. Their merchandise includes hats, shirts, cups, pop-sockets, and stickers.

A typical day for them involves checking sales and online activity, as well as managing their Instagram account. They express the thrill of closing deals and the sacrifices they make, like missing out on social events. Their parents helped with website development, and the brothers reflect on the valuable lessons they have learned, such as the importance of securely attaching fins to surfboards.

Regarding their future aspirations, Ethan wants to pursue surfing professionally and reach the World Surf League (WSL), while Merritt aims to become a basketball player, hockey goalie, or soccer player.

ZAlphas and The Metaverse

The Metaverse is swiftly gaining traction among the tech-savvy demographic, particularly Gen Z and Gen Alpha (ZAlphas). According to a survey conducted by Dubit, a children's media and technology agency, 81% of kids aged 6–12 have heard of the metaverse, and 59% would like to live there. Kids are excited about the possibilities that the metaverse could bring, such as being able to do things that are impossible in the real world.

ZAlphas spend about 30 hours every week watching videos. This is three times more than their gaming time and five times more than their non-video internet use. Metaverse TV could become places like 'channels' where different ideas come together, or smaller spaces with a strong brand. For Generation Z and Alpha, though, just watching TV might seem boring compared to playing games like Among Us, Fortnite, or Roblox.

One of the key features that kids would like to see in the metaverse is customisation. They want to be able to create their own avatars, personalise their environment, and make choices that affect their virtual experience. Gen ZAlpha kids want to be able to express themselves through their avatars and have the freedom to be whoever they want to be. Big brands let Gen ZAlphas buy 'skins' with names like Nike, Adidas, and Under Armour for their game characters. Moreover, Nike has created 'Airtopia', a special place in the metaverse just for kids. Also a children's fashion brand called Balabala recently joined the metaverse too, and they've made a lifelike digital brand ambassador named 'Rainy'. Even big kids' brands like Hasbro and Mattel have started their own metaverse adventures.[51]

Another important aspect of the metaverse for Gen ZAlpha kids is socialising. They want to be able to interact with other users, make friends, and have fun together. This includes both synchronous and asynchronous communication, with some kids preferring real-time chat while others enjoy leaving messages for their friends to discover later. However, safety is also a concern for kids, and they want to ensure that they are interacting with other users who are their age and have similar interests.

In addition to customisation and socialisation, kids also want to have a sense of purpose in the metaverse. They want to be able to achieve goals, complete quests, and earn rewards. This gives them a sense of accomplishment and helps to keep them engaged in the virtual world.

Finally, kids want the metaverse to be accessible and inclusive. They want to be able to access the metaverse on a variety of devices, including mobile phones and tablets. They also want to see a diverse range of characters and experiences in the metaverse, including different cultures, abilities, and backgrounds.

Overall, the metaverse represents an exciting new frontier for kids, offering endless possibilities for exploration, creativity, and socialising. However, it is important for creators and developers to listen to the needs and desires of kids to ensure that the Metaverse is a safe, engaging, and inclusive space for all users.[48]

'If a product designed for kids in the metaverse enters the market, it should emphasise the safety measures it has in place. Without these safeguards, parents – who are the decision-makers – might not approve of the metaverse, no matter how promising it seems,'

explains Krishna Iyer.[53]

Consequences of the Metaverse

The metaverse is a simulated environment that brings physical and virtual realities together. There are many promising benefits of the metaverse, such as immersive user experiences, but it also has some negative consequences as well, which have remained relatively unexplored. Some of the impacts are discussed below:

Psychological and Physiological Impacts

Recent research has shed light on the potential adverse effects on mental and physical wellbeing resulting from the absence of pleasurable real-life experiences within virtual environments. These findings underscore the significant impact that the metaverse can have on both psychological and physiological health. Prolonged and excessive use of Extended Reality (XR) devices, in particular, has been identified as a potential source of concern. Such prolonged usage carries the risk of addiction and can detrimentally affect users' vision when worn for extended periods.

Frequent engagement with XR devices has been linked to the development of blurring the boundaries between the virtual and real worlds. This visual impairment can lead to difficulties in distinguishing between the two realms, potentially compromising users' ability to navigate and function effectively in their physical surroundings. Moreover, the regular and excessive use of these devices has been associated with heightened stress levels, further exacerbating the potential long-term consequences. The addictive nature of the metaverse can generate traumatic effects, amplifying the impact on individuals' wellbeing.

These findings raise important concerns about the potential risks associated with excessive immersion in virtual environments. While the metaverse presents unique opportunities for exploration and engagement, it is essential to strike a balance that prioritises the users' overall health and wellbeing. Responsible and mindful use of XR devices, coupled with periodic breaks and moderation, can help mitigate the potential negative effects.

Moral and Legal Issues

The metaverse, as it currently stands, lacks comprehensive rules and regulations aimed at safeguarding its users from various forms of misconduct and illegal activities. Identity theft, cyberbullying, flirting, harassment, racism, and other threats can occur within the metaverse, and while these incidents may appear to be confined to the virtual realm, the subsequent traumatic effects experienced by individuals are undeniably real. Such issues have the potential to undermine global cultural and ethical systems, warranting urgent attention.

While the psychological impact of these incidents may not fall directly within the jurisdiction of legal frameworks, the physiological consequences can be more readily addressed by governments and companies. Physical harm caused by metaverse-related activities can be regulated through established laws and industry standards. For instance, measures can be implemented to ensure user safety, such as enforcing guidelines on appropriate behaviour, developing robust reporting mechanisms, and implementing moderation systems to swiftly address and penalise offenders.

However, it is important to recognise that the metaverse's unique nature presents challenges in effectively regulating and mitigating these issues. The metaverse encompasses a vast virtual landscape with countless users and interactions, making it difficult to monitor and control every aspect of user behaviour. The sheer scale and complexity of the metaverse demands collaborative efforts between governments, technology companies, and user communities to develop comprehensive solutions.

To address the lack of protection against scams, identity theft, and other forms of illegal activities within the metaverse, it is crucial to establish clear legal frameworks that define and penalise such offences. This would serve as a deterrent and provide avenues for victims to seek justice. Additionally, raising awareness about the potential risks and educating users on responsible and ethical behaviour within the metaverse can empower individuals to protect themselves and contribute to a safer virtual environment.

In conclusion, while the metaverse currently lacks robust regulations to safeguard users from various threats, it is imperative that measures be put in place to address issues such as scams, cyberbullying, harassment, and racism. By combining legal frameworks, industry standards, community guidelines, and user education, we can work towards creating a metaverse that prioritises the wellbeing and safety of its users, both psychologically and physiologically.

Security Issues

The nature of advanced technological applications inherently gives rise to security considerations. In this regard, the metaverse presents unique challenges as it provides developers and marketers with an array of user behaviour tracking possibilities. These include but are not limited to eye-tracking, monitoring pupil movements, analysing geometric movements, observing physical gestures, and more. Through the metaverse, a lot of personal data like biometric data, emotional behaviour of the users, their walking pattern etc. can be collected. Misuse of this data can lead to serious trouble like fraud, identity theft, cyber-hacking, or may even create a physical threat to innocent users (due to a breach of residential data). What is more difficult than the breach is actually proving that there has been a data breach through cyber attack. Specific knowledge and skills are needed to protect the users of this breach and compensation will be much more difficult.[38]

Many exciting entertainment, education and social interaction opportunities can be found on the metaverse. However, with these benefits come a few risks especially for children. Kids are usually more vulnerable to forms of online harm, which is why it is crucial to implement safety measures to safeguard your and your family's wellbeing in the metaverse.

One of the primary concerns raised by Ffiske[39] is the potential of online predators that can manipulate and exploit kids using virtual spaces. Children that use the metaverse and other virtual spaces interact with other users thus increasing the risk of encountering people with malicious intentions. Ffiske suggested the need for powerful moderation systems or tools for auto identification and prevention of such instances to ensure a safe environment for children.

Kids may overshare their personal information while interacting in virtual spaces. This could lead to different forms of privacy breaches including identity theft. It is crucial for parents to implement privacy controls. They should also teach their children about safe online practices to help reduce the risks involved. Their guidance, involvement and supervision is necessary to ensure their children's safety in the metaverse. Collaboration between parents, platform providers, and regulators is necessary to establish guidelines and standards that prioritise child safety.

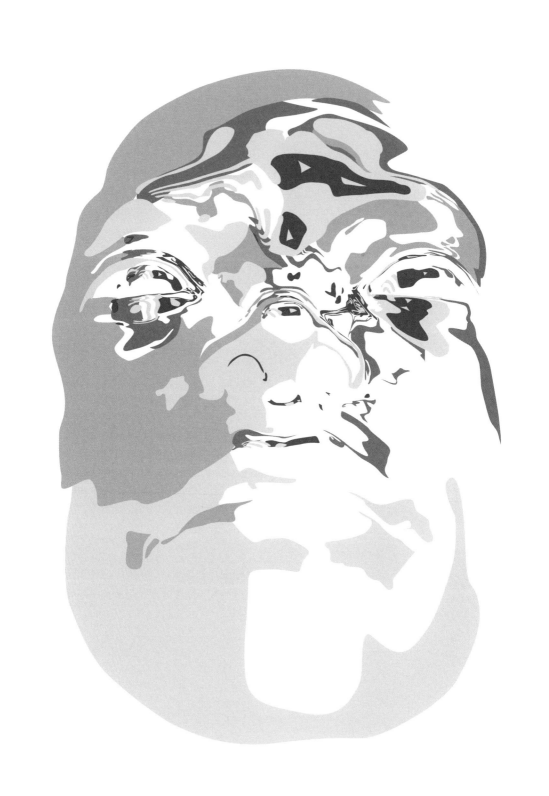

Chapter 6:
Data Privacy, Laws and Advertisements

Communication in the digital age has raised new challenges. With the development of modern information technologies, new kinds of violence have appeared, such as cyberbullying and humiliation or harassment using smartphones.

Anna Branding[40] recently reported such a privacy breach incident involving Amazon's Ring camera system used for spying on customers. Ring cameras are home security devices that make it convenient for the users to check on their properties remotely. Branding reported an incident where a hacker hacked a Ring camera installed in Amazon and used this for invading the privacy of the customers. There was a vulnerability in the software of that Ring camera which allowed the incident to happen. The hacker used that weakness in his favour and gained access to the live video feed. He not only invaded customers' privacy but also gained access to their personal lives which is a serious security breach.

Through her blog, Anna Branding has emphasised the importance of regularly updating and securing the connected devices for protection against intrusions. The incident also highlighted the need to be cautious while installing and using such devices, reviewing privacy settings on a regular basis and setting up strong passwords. The security and privacy of smart home devices must be taken seriously. Especially when there are kids involved in such situations.

Here are some laws to protect your kids from exploitation on social media platforms.

Child Labour Laws and Coogan's Law

Labour laws do not extend to 'Kidfluencers' due to their activities occurring within the private setting of a home and on platforms where parents voluntarily participate. Their actions are not classified as 'work' as there is no employer-employee relationship, and their presence on camera is considered ordinary behaviour rather than a 'performance'.

While these regulations exist within the child entertainment industry, they rarely apply to 'Kidfluencers'. Coogan's Law was established following the experience of child actor Jackie Coogan, who realised at age 21 that his earnings from his acting career had been spent by his parents. This law mandates that parents establish a safeguarded trust account to save a portion of the child actor's wages until they turn 18. This new law also upholds the 'right to be forgotten', meaning that social media platforms must remove child content upon the child's request. Under this law, parental government authorisation is required before a child engages in online activities that resemble a 'labour relation'.

The subsequent points highlight the positive aspects of children engaging with the social media world, including learning entrepreneurial skills and business development.

Moving forward, while social media platforms like YouTube have committed to combat child exploitation and protect child privacy, the mechanisms for accountability remain limited. While respecting parental autonomy, their decisions should always prioritise the child's best interests.

Governments might consider implementing work permits for 'Kidfluencers' to monitor profit generated from children's social media activity by parents or guardians. This would ensure children are not financially exploited and discourage parents from such activities if financial gains are less likely.

Creators of child-focused content could collaborate to establish online community mechanisms for accountability and information sharing.

Legal provisions could follow examples from France and California, requiring trusts to be set up for 'Kidfluencers' who are part of profit-generating social media profiles.[41]

Given the active online presence of ZAlphas, advertising becomes a sensitive matter for companies. Some parents argue that advertising to children is inappropriate and should be entirely prohibited. However, in today's context, such an approach is neither feasible nor advisable. Brands, as we've observed, play a significant and meaningful role in the lives of ZAlphas. They bring excitement, entertainment, education, and information. We believe that products can be marketed to children as long as strict criteria are met.

The Responsible Advertising and Children (RAC) programme assists brands in identifying these criteria. It brings together a global community of nearly a thousand individuals with a vested interest in the intersection of marketing and children. The RAC's objective is to lead globally by advocating good practices in marketing communication to children. This initiative involves ongoing dialogues and engagements with policymakers, society, and parents. RAC ensures its members are informed about the latest developments, interacts with policymakers and stakeholders on key concerns, identifies emerging trends, devises potential industry and company solutions, monitors member activities to prevent potential issues, and drives 'beyond compliance' initiatives that safeguard companies' ability to connect with younger consumers.

Other Key Privacy Laws for Children

COPPA enforces specific mandates on operators of websites or online services aimed at children under 13 years old, as well as operators of other online services who are aware that they are collecting personal information from children under 13. This law applies universally to both children and adults, incorporating specific provisions tailored to child protection. The additional safeguards for children stem from their limited familiarity with the risks, implications, and safeguards concerning their personal and public data.

Despite the headway achieved through these regulations, variations still exist across states and countries. Furthermore, some parents may inadvertently disregard these laws to grant permission for their children to access various online tools before they reach the age of 13. Sharing personal information such as full name, birth date, phone number, and location can leave one vulnerable to data theft. It is crucial to refrain from sharing this information about oneself or others with anyone. Additionally, individuals should consider the potential consequences of their online posts on their future prospects. What may seem amusing or trendy now could negatively impact future career opportunities.

It's vital to remind children that whatever they share online remains accessible indefinitely. Limiting the audience for shared information and configuring privacy and security settings online is important. The National Cyber Security Alliance offers direct links to some of the most popular online platforms. Devices like smartwatches are garnering increased attention due to their potential security vulnerabilities.

Data Privacy Tips for Children

A first one, when browsing, is to only access secure websites. A recommended step is to employ 'HTTPS Everywhere', a browser extension available for Firefox, Chrome, and Opera that encrypts communications with major websites, enhancing browsing security. It is advised to refrain from using the 'remember me' feature on public computers.

Secondly, to address the safety concerns in the metaverse for example, brands should take a proactive approach to safety. This should involve creating clear policies around online harassment and hate speech, as well as implementing privacy protections to safeguard user data. Brands should also consider partnering with organisations that specialise in digital safety and promoting responsible use of the metaverse. They should prioritise transparency and user control. This should involve giving users the ability to control their data and how it is used, as well as providing clear information about the risks and benefits of using the metaverse. By taking a proactive approach to safety and prioritising transparency and user control, brands can help to ensure that the metaverse is a safe and positive space for users.[43]

Lastly, privacy regulations such as the European General Data Protection Regulation (GDPR), the United States Federal Children's Online Privacy Protection Act (COPPA) of 1998, and California's recently enacted Privacy Rights Act have played a pivotal role in advancing data protection measures. However, parents still bear the primary responsibility for safeguarding their children's online privacy, encompassing both reputation and consumer privacy.

Advertisements:
Watch-Outs for Children's Wellbeing

Aside from laws and privacy tips, there are some negative impacts of advertisements to be considered. We have outlined some negative effects from ads on children's wellbeing below as follows:

- Induces eating disorders – Advertisements frequently employ young and attractive individuals to endorse beauty products. Such ads could instil self-consciousness in children about their appearance and contribute to the development of a negative body image.

- Entices children to attempt dangerous stunts – Inexperienced children might misconstrue these portrayals as real and attempt risky stunts at home.
- Contributes to obesity – Advertisements propagate the misguided idea that consuming specific beverages or fast food equates to success or happiness. Under the influence of such ads, children may exhibit a preference for unhealthy foods, thereby fostering obesity.
- Fosters adverse emotions – Children may succumb to the influence of these commercials, leading them to compare themselves with peers or harbour a sense of superiority or inferiority.
- Encourages impulsive purchasing – Prolonged exposure to these advertisements might incline children towards impulsive buying, irrespective of their actual need for the product.
- Cultivates a penchant for high-end and pricey items – Through advertisements, children might develop an affinity for branded clothing, shoes, and other upscale products.[59]

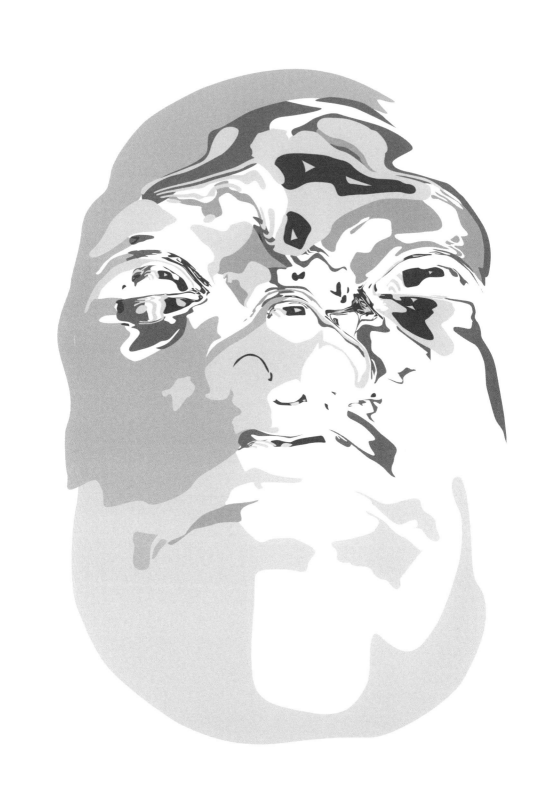

Conclusion

Kids all around the globe have observed their parents adapting to remote work during lockdowns, potentially shaping a new approach to work-life balance. This allows employees to work from home while preserving quality time with family and loves ones. While this young generation had to endure lockdowns, isolating themselves to protect older generations, they've also experienced significant sacrifices. It led to missed milestones like graduations and birthdays, impacting the young generation's social experiences.

The emergence of Generation ZAlpha brings unique challenges and opportunities. Being the first generation raised with technology as an omnipresent force, they are tech-savvy, witnessing the positive environmental impact of reduced travel. Yet, concerns linger about over-reliance on technology – resulting in mental health, anxiety, addiction and social isolation issues. Parents play a crucial role in mitigating tech's negative effects on their children's mental health. Setting screen time limits, encouraging diverse activities, and modelling healthy tech habits are essential in order for parents to foster a healthy tech relationship for their children. The rapid pace of this new environment also raises concerns about its impact on memory, as voice assistants like Siri or Alexa might have adverse effects.

They aspire to financial freedom, using mobile apps like Robinhood for investments in stocks and cryptocurrencies, and are deeply connected through social media. Furthermore, they acknowledge the emergence of non-fungible tokens (NFTs) and their integration into their lives in the years to come. This generation's wealth is projected to be substantial, but they'll spend longer duration in education, enter the workforce later, start families at a later stage and seek individual rewards. Remote work is natural for them given their upbringing in a tech-immersed world, but workplace structures must adapt. ZAlphas won't merely follow a set curriculum but will seek specialisation in various subjects and niches. Gen ZAlpha dreams of helping others or having fun, with regional distinctions in career preferences. They prioritise recognition, societal benefits, and individuality.

Youngsters perceive phones as essential. They view technology as a tool for transformative change and gravitate towards companies aligned with their goals and societal benefits. They prioritise being treated as individuals rather than just workers, and desire recognition exceeding prior generations. The future appears promising for them. Nevertheless, it's crucial to acquaint them with the realities of the world to manage expectations. Previous generations must develop skills enabling seamless collaboration with Gen Z and Gen Alpha in professional and educational settings. The technological upbringing of both generations is a positive indicator of the innovations they'll create.

I am often asked where I see the difference between Generation Z and ZAlpha. I also see it mostly in how the latter generations view reality. What they experience in the online world is a real reality for them. If they meet a well-known influencer in a Roblox space, they were really there with him or her. It is the older generations that see a difference in that, not the youngest generation.

Where Gen Z still demands that the digital experience approaches the real experience, Gen ZAlpha will be the generation that demands that the real experience offers at least as much as it does in the digital world.

When it comes to marketing to Gen ZAlpha, or, engaging with them, below are some key summarising thoughts and behaviours of Generation ZAlpha that must be considered. These include:

1. **Tech-savviness:** Generation ZAlpha are growing up in an age where technology is ubiquitous and is increasingly becoming a central part of their lives. With a majority of children in this age group having access to digital devices such as tablets and smartphones, digital marketing and advertising may be a key way to reach this generation.

2. **Social and environmental awareness:** Generation ZAlpha are more aware of social and environmental issues than previous generations, and this awareness is likely to shape their values and beliefs as they grow up. Companies that take a socially and environmentally responsible approach to their products and services may be more appealing to this generation.

3. **Educational and developmental focus:** Generation ZAlpha's parents prioritise their children's education and wellbeing, and marketing messages that emphasise the educational and developmental benefits of products and services may be more effective with this generation.

4. **Diversity and inclusion:** Generation ZAlpha is considered to be the most diverse generation ever, and marketers who are able to create inclusive and culturally relevant messaging may be more appealing to this generation.

5. **Emerging technology industries:** Generation ZAlpha is expected to have a significant impact on the economy, particularly in emerging technology industries such as artificial intelligence and virtual reality. Companies in these industries may have a unique opportunity to market to this generation and appeal to their tech-savvy nature.[61]

Finally, don't forget that this micro-generation has inherited their Gen Y or Millennial parents' hedonic values, however ZAlphas definitely want to and surely will form their own values based on their lived experiences. The fact that they grew up in an environment where they can design, create and make themselves (thanks to technological advancements), they know it's possible to see the results of their actions. This micro-generation might barely be out of diapers, but they mostly are so ready to fix, tweak, improve and take daily life, influencing, brands and everything in between to the next level – all in a humane and authentic way!

Curious about what the future holds? Allow us to introduce you to Generation Beta. According to the trend forecasting agency WGSN, the next generation on the horizon are the Betas. Born between 2025 and 2040, these youngsters will be the offspring of a generation deeply entrenched in online living, but more notably, they'll be the first to embrace an AI-driven existence for their learning, play, and work. Watch this space!

[1]   A. Buller, E. Rhodes and H. Friend, 'The Zalpha Reckoning', LS:N Global, 02 12 2021.

[2]   I. Batada, 'Generation Alpha', 2022.

[3]   R. Huntley, 'The big idea: why the generation gap isn't as wide as you think', 2023.

[4]   B. Duffy, Generations: Does When You're Born Shape Who You Are?, 2021.

[5]   S. K. Bannon, Director, Generation Zero. [Film]. 2010.

[6]   T. Ling, 'Generation Alpha: 'more Gen Z than Gen Z'', 2021.

[7]   S. Bregel, ''Sharenting'' is problematic. This app gives parents an alternative way to post about their kids', 13 April 2023.

[8]   K. Idelson, 'Why Reaching Gen Z and Gen Alpha Is the Holy Grail for Entertainment Marketers', variety.com, 19 Apr. 2023.

[9]   J. Howarth, 'Generation Alpha: Statistics, Data and Trends (2023)', explodingtopics.com, 2023.

[10]   A. Gregory, 'Primary-age children's screen time went up by 83 minutes a day during pandemic – study', The Guardian, 24 06 2022. [Online]. Available: https://www.theguardian.com/society/2022/jun/24/primary-age-children-screen-time-went-up-83-minutes-day-pandemic. [Accessed 14 09 2022].

[11]   C. Beer, '2 years of Covid: what's changed?', GWI., 22 03 2022. [Online]. Available: https://blog.gwi.com/chart-of-the-week/2-years-from-Covid/. [Accessed 14 09 2022].

[12]   V. McKeever, 'Isolation during Covid pandemic has delayed kids' social skills, new study says', 04 04 2022. [Online]. Available: https://www.cnbc.com/2022/04/04/uk-study-kids-struggle-with-writing-and-speech-after-the-pandemic.html. [Accessed 15 09 2022].

[13]   A. Hernandez, 'Toddlers are aces at touch screens, according to a new report', 2023.

[14]   D. P. Keating, 'The Youth Stress Pandemic: Social Distress, Not Social Media', 12 07 2022. [Online]. Available: https://www.psychology-today.com/intl/blog/stressful-lives/202207/the-youth-stress-pandemic-social-distress-not-social-media. [Accessed 15 09 2022].

[15]   J. Perkel, 'Why Many Children Are Suffering Today', 20 07 2022. [Online]. Available: https://www.psychologytoday.com/intl/blog/21st-century-childhood/202207/why-many-children-are-suffering-today. [Accessed 15 09 2022].

[16]   M. W. Moyer, 'The Covid generation: how is the pandemic affecting kids' brains?', 12 01 2022. [Online]. Available: https://www.nature.com/articles/d41586-022-00027-4. [Accessed 15 09 2022].

[17]   'Covid-19: Five crises facing children after 2 years of pandemic', Save the Children, 2022.

[18]   V. Trifonova and S. Moran, 'Generation Alpha: The Real Picture', gwi.com, 2022.

[19]   'Gen Alpha: The next economic force', Caxton & CTP Printers and Publishers Ltd., 2022.

[20]   A. Kelso, 'Apparently Gen Alpha really likes McDonald's', nrn.com, 2023.

[21]   D. Robson, 'The biggest myths of the teenage brain', 2022.

[22]   S. Phillips, 'Dove campaign examines 'cost of beauty' for youth mental health', thred.com, 5 May 2023.

[23]   S. Bharanidharan, 'Exploring a new niche for kids career development content', kidscreen.com, 2023.

[24]   J. Timperley, 'Do people yet to be born have climate change rights?', bbc.com, 2023.

[25]   S. Gutelle, '20% of 18-to-24-year-olds use TikTok as a news source', TubeFilter, 14 June 2023.

[26]   S. Phillips, 'Compassion fatigue: is Gen Z numb to tragedy?', thred.com, 21 12 2022.

[27]   'What is Generation Alpha, and why is it the most influential generation in CX?', Infobip, 17 March 2022. [Online]. Available: https://www.thedrum.com/profile/infobip/news/gen-alpha-the-most-influential-generation-for-cx. [Accessed 14 September 2022].

[28]   D. Wachaya, 'Why Gen Z is the driving force behind Africa's tech advancements', thred.com, 22 Feb 2023.

[29]   M. Klein, 'A_Roundtable: Gen Z Online: Control, Expression, Connection', 2023.

[30]   J. V. d. Bergh, K. Pallini and S. V. Oerle, 'Gen Z x Metaverse [EUR infographic]', 2022.

[31]   BBC, bbc.co.uk.

[32]   Y. Raz-Fridman, 'Roblox Earnings: Takeaways', intometamedia.com, 2023.

[33]   V. Tangermann, 'Mom Horrified by What Her Kids Are Seeing in Roblox', 2023.

[34]   hoomale.com.

[35]   US 'Gen Alpha study' , Razorfish , GWI and The Pineapple Lounge, August 2023.

[36]   'How has the pandemic affected children's screen time?', weforum.org, 11 03 2022. [Online]. Available: https://www.weforum.org/agenda/2022/05/pandemic-children-screen-time/. [Accessed 14 09 2022].

[37]   N. Al-Sibai, 'Scientists Find Something Strange In Brain Scans Of Kids Hooked On Social Media', 2023.

[38]   Yogesh K. Dwivedi, Nir Kshetri, Laurie Hughes, Nripendra P. Rana, Abdullah M. Baabdullah, Arpan Kumar Kar, Alex Koohang, Samuel Ribeiro-Navarrete, Nina Belei, Janarthanan Balakrishnan, Sriparna Basu, Abhishek Behl, Gareth H. Davies and Vincent Dutot, 'Exploring the Darkverse: A Multi-Perspective Analysis of the Negative', Information Systems Frontiers, 2023.

[39]   T. Ffiske, 'Safety experts query allowing minors into Horizon Worlds', 2023.

[40] A. Branding, 'Amazon's Ring cameras were used to spy on customers', *MalwareBytes*, 1 June 2023.

[41] V. C. Cordeiro, 'Kidfluencers' and Social Media: The Evolution of Child Exploitation in the Digital Age', Posted in Children's Rights, Explotation, Freedom, Labour, 2021.

[42] C. Wisniewski, 'Digital Marketing and Our Digital Reckoning', 14 July 2022. [Online]. Available: https://www.psychologytoday.com/intl/blog/younoob-thoughts-digital-growing-pains/202207/digital-marketing-and-our-digital-reckoning. [Accessed 18 September 2022].

[43] T. I. Family, 'What are the key metaverse safety concerns and how can brands respond?', 2022.

[44] 'How to protect your child's data and privacy in 2021', 26 January 2021. [Online]. Available: https://www.qustodio.com/en/blog/protect-child-data-privacy/. [Accessed 18 September 2022].

[45] R. Yadhunath, 'Why Children Need to Be Taught Data Literacy', 22 July 2020. [Online]. Available: https://medium.com/age-of-awareness/why-children-need-to-be-taught-data-literacy-77a9db2c2599. [Accessed 18 September 2022].

[46] S. Ghai, L. Magis-Weinberg, M. Stoilova, S. Livingstone and A. Orben, 'Social media and adolescent wellbeing in the Global South', *Current Opinion in Psychology*, vol. 46, 2022.

[47] M. Miller, 'Social Media and the Neuroscience of Predictive Processing'.

[48] C. Watson, 'What do kids want from the metaverse?', kidscreen.com, 2023.

[49] S. Stubbins, 'Virtual parenthood: On children and the metaverse', harpersbazaar.com.au, 2022.

[50] D. Kleeman, 'Kids have Kickstarted the Metaverse', 03 June 2021. [Online]. Available: https://techonomy.com/kids-have-kickstarted-the-metaverse/. [Accessed 18 September 2022].

[51] A. Lapin, 'The Future of Gen Alpha and Sports Lies in the Metaverse', 25 Oct 2021. [Online]. Available: https://musebycl.io/sports/future-gen-alpha-and-sports-lies-metaverse. [Accessed 2022 September 2022].

[52] N. Reed, 'What Are Kids Doing in the Metaverse?', commonsensemedia.org, 2022.

[53] T. Shaikh, 'Brands are wooing kids in the Metaverse, but how safe is the 'Phygital' world for the young ones?', Mumbai, 2022.

[54] 'Children, competition and the metaverse', 21 Aug 2022. [Online]. Available: https://www.bennettinstitute.cam.ac.uk/blog/children-competition-and-the-metaverse/. [Accessed 18 Sep 2022].

[55] W. Meers, 'Roblox's metaverse is overhyped, a new report suggests', 17 Aug 2022. [Online]. Available: https://www.pcgamesn.com/roblox/metaverse-overhyped. [Accessed 18 Sep 2022].

[56] S. Moran, 'What Gen Alpha's habits tell us about the future of gaming', 24 May 2022. [Online]. Available: https://blog.gwi.com/chart-of-the-week/gen-alphas-habits-future-of-gaming/. [Accessed 18 Sep 2022].

[57] A. Bhagi, 'Metaverse for kids – Preparing children for a creator's economy and a mixed reality future', 26 Apr 2022. [Online]. Available: https://timesofindia.indiatimes.com/blogs/voices/metaverse-for-kids-preparing-children-for-a-creators-economy-and-a-mixed-reality-future/. [Accessed 18 Sep 2022].

[58] J. Katz, 'Gaming in the metaverse: online safety in another dimension', 10 Aug 2022. [Online]. Available: https://www.public.io/blog-post/gaming-in-the-metaverse-online-safety-in-another-dimension. [Accessed 19 Sep 2022].

[59] N. J. Patel, 'Nina Jane Patel on a safe, responsible Metaverse', 2022.

[60] S. BREGEL, 'Gen Alpha is tech savvy and growing up fast, but their parents worry about their mental health', fastcompany.com, 2023.

[61] J. Chodakowsky, 'Marketing to Generation Alpha, the Newest and Youngest Cohort', ana.net, 2022.

[62] G. Atwal, 'Meet Generation Alpha: The Shrewdest Luxury Consumers Ever?', 2021.

[63] A. Viens, 'An Investing Megatrend: How Demographics and Social Changes are Shaping the Future', visualcapitalist.com, 2022.

[64] E. Santiago, 'If Gen Z Changed the Game for Marketers, What Will Gen Alpha Be Like?', 2019.

[65] N. Reed, 'What Are Kids Doing in the Metaverse?', 2022.

[66] M. Tamashiro, 'Who is the Metaverse generation?', 2022.

[67] G. Yalcuk, 'Why Generation Alpha Is The Future of Humanity', 2022.

[68] S. Perez, 'Kids and teens now spend more time watching TikTok than YouTube, new data shows', 2022.

[69] M. Brito, 'Understanding Gen Alpha: Stats, Trends & Insights for 2023', britopian.com, 2022.

[70] P. Singh, S. Sahadev, C. J. Oates and P. Alevizou, 'Pro-environmental behavior in families: A reverse socialization perspective', *Journal of Business Research*, vol. 115, no. July, pp. 110-121, 2020.

[71] 'Gen Z cares about sustainability more than anyone else – and is starting to make others feel the same', 2022.

[72] 'How Amsterdam's youth - or Alpha generation

- is reimagining the city's future', 2021.

[73] C. W. Rudolph and H. Zacher, 'Considering Generations From a Lifespan Developmental Perspective', *Work, Aging and Retirement*, vol. 3, no. 2, pp. 113-129, 2017.

[74] I. Leijen, H. v. Herk and A. Bardi, 'Individual and generational value change in an adult population, a 12-year longitudinal panel study', *Scientific Report*, 2023.

[75] C. W. Rudolph, R. S. Rauvola, D. P. Costanza and H. Zacher, 'Generations and Generational Differences: Debunking Myths in Organisational Science and Practice and Paving New Paths Forward', *Nature Public Health Emergency Collection*, 2021.

[76] J. Braune, 'Talking About My Generation: Understanding Generational Marketing', 2021.

[77] H. Fletcher, 'Generation ALpha: Preparing for the future Consumer', 2019. [Online]. Available: https://www.wundermanthompson.com/insight/generation-alpha-2019. [Accessed 14 September 2022].

[78] T. Chatfield, 'The attention economy'.

[79] D. Winter, 'Generation Alpha: Everything Brands Need To Know', shopify.com, 11 Nov 2022.

[80] M. Debczak, 'These Revised Guidelines Redefine Birth Years and Classifications for Millennials, Gen Z, and Gen Alpha', 2023.

[81] pico.com, https://www.pico.com/en/work/2021-escape-room-experience-at-midea-pop-up-store.

[82] N. Melcher, 'Deep Dive: Early Metaverse Players – Data on Demographics, Socializing, Playing, & Spending', 2022.

[83] R. Horijk, 'Peripheral Consumer Insights: Targeting Gen Z (and Younger) Makes for Lifelong Fans, But Older Generations Present a Massive Opportunity', 2022.

[84] M. Harrison, 'Certain Kids Can Get Heart Attacks From Gaming, Doctors Say', 2022.

[85] J. Cannon, 'Marketers to focus on Gen Z in 2023 with dollars moving to TikTok, raw approach to creative', 2023.

[86] W. Europe, 'The Next Generation is Already Plugged In – Here's How Their Millennial Parents Feel About It', 2022.

[87] Poole Thought Leadership, 'Meet the mini-millennials: Generation Alpha', 2021.

[88] M. Guillen, 'Why we are heading toward a post-generational society according to the dean of Wharton', fastcompany.com, 2023.

[89] J. Howarth, 'Generation Alpha: Statistics, Data and Trends 2023' 2023. [Online]. Available: https://explodingtopics.com/blog/generation-alpha-stats. [Accessed 18 September 2023].

[90] V. Troy, 'Read of the Week: Gen Alpha's Development Delay' 2022. [Online]. Available: https://www.canvas8.com/blog/2022/april/read-of-the-week-gen-alphas-developmental-delay. [Accessed 18 September 2023].

[91] D. Reuter, 'How brands can connect with Gen Alpha' 2023. [Online]. Available: https://www.entrepreneur.com/business-news/how-brands-can-connect-with-generation-alpha/447657. [Accessed 18 September 2023].

[92] S. Jordahn, 'Counterspace's Children's Courtroom Installation' 2021. [Online]. Available: https://www.dezeen.com/2021/07/01/counterspace-childrens-courtroom-sumayya-vally-video-interview/ [Accessed 19 September 2023].

[93] C. Smith, 'Trend Hunter Dives into the Importance of Micro-Generation Groups' 2022. [Online]. Available: https://www.trendhunter.com/trends/micro-generations. [Accessed 19 September 2023].

[94] D. Eunice Narciso, 'Step up your Game: Marketing to Generation Alpha' 2023. [Online]. Available: https://debutify.com/blog/marketing-to-generation-alpha/#:~:text=Lego%20has%20been%20a%20beloved,parents%2C%20and%20young%20Lego%20enthusiasts. [Accessed 19 September 2023].

[95] D. Griner, 'Kids Can Use This Ad Tracker to Pester Their Parents Into Shopping Sustainably' 2021. [Online]. Available: https://www.adweek.com/programmatic/kids-can-use-this-ad-tracker-to-pester-their-parents-into-shopping-sustainably/ [Accessed 19 September 2023].

[96] J. De Wit, 'Ge(n)eratie', 2023.

[97] Canvas8, 'Calm X Disney aims to tackle anxiety among Gen Alphas' 2023. [Online]. Available: https://www.canvas8.com/library/signals/2023/08/16/calm-x-disney-aims-to-tackle-anxiety-amongst-genalpha. [Accessed 21 September 2023].

[98] Canvas8, 'Milka Brings Accessibility to Easter for Blind Children' 2023. [Online]. Available: https://www.canvas8.com/library/signals/2023/03/29/milka-brings-accessibility-to-easter-for-blind-children. [Accessed 21 September 2023].

[99] Canvas8, 'Goalsetter: financial education platform for families' 2022. [Online]. Available: https://www.canvas8.com/library/case-studies/2022/11/07/goalsetter-financial-education-platform-for-families. [Accessed 21 September 2023].

[100] Canvas8, 'TikTok Daily Limit Addresses Teen Screen Time Concerns' 2023. [Online]. Available: https://www.canvas8.com/library/signals/2023/03/08/tiktok-daily-limit-addresses-teen-screen-time-concerns. [Accessed 22 September 2023]

[101] Barnados, 'Cost Of Living Crisis: Impact on Children' 2022. [Online]. Available: https://

www.barnardos.ie/news/2022/june/cost-of-living-crisis-impact-on-children. [Accessed 22 September 2023].

[102] B. Auxier, M. Anderson, A. Perrin, E. Turner, 'Parenting Children in The Age of Screens' 2020. [Online]. Available: https://www.pewresearch.org/internet/2020/07/28/parenting-children-in-the-age-of-screens/. [Accessed 22 September 2023].

[103] GWI 'Generation Alpha: The New Kids of America' 2022. [Online]. Available: https://www.gwi.com/reports/gen-alpha-us. [Accessed 22 September 2023].

[104] Canvas8, 'Fenty Beauty Goes to The Metaverse With Roblox' 2023. [Online]. Available: https://www.canvas8.com/library/signals/2023/07/10/fenty-beauty-goes-to-the-metaverse-with-roblox. [Accessed 22 September 2023]

[105] Canvas8, 'Snack Uses AI Avatars to Screen for Dates' 2023. [Online]. Available: https://www.canvas8.com/library/signals/2023/04/05/snack-uses-ai-avatars-to-screen-for-dates. [Accessed 22 September 2023]

[106] Uhrig, S. Generation Alpha: Diapers, Training Wheels and Artificial Intelligence.

[107] Chromey, Rick. 2020. GenTech: An American Story of Technology, Change, and Who We Really Are (1900-Present). New York: Morgan James Publishing.